THE DARWEN COUNTY HISTORY SERIES

A History of LINCOLNSHIRE

Stewart Bennett

Phillimore

1999

Published by
PHILLIMORE & CO. LTD.
Shopwyke Manor Barn, Chichester, West Sussex

First published, 1970
Second edition, 1985
Third edition, 1999

ISBN 1 86077 089 4

Printed and bound in Great Britain by
BUTLER AND TANNER LTD.
Frome, Somerset

Contents

List of Illustrations

Frontispiece: Map of Lincolnshire, *c.*1840

List of Colour Illustrations

Acknowledgements

Appleby Coaches, 74; Paul Dobson, 96; FLARE/David Vale, 14, 30; Heritage Lincolnshire/Christopher Cruickshank, I, II, II, X, XI, 10, 45; Institution of Engineers, 80; Malcolm Johnson, 107, 110; Lincolnshire County Council, V, VII, VIII, XII, XIII, 6, 11, 16, 21, 22, 44; Lincolnshire Archives Office/ Lincolnshire County Council, 93; North Lincolnshire Museum, 4, 55, 81, 109, 113; Jane Robson, for all the drawings; R.C. Russell, 64; Usher Gallery/Lincolnshire County Council, IV, front cover; David Vale, 27; Dave Watt, 2, 5, 12, 20, 26, 28, 29, 36, 40, 54, 69, 74, 92, 106.

Introduction

This book is for all those with an interest in the history of Lincolnshire. The county has a history that is unique, due to its position in Britain, its long coastline, its diverse geology and topography and its size as the second largest in England. These factors have impacted on man's activities through the centuries to the present day. To write a continuous history of a county as large and diverse as Lincolnshire is a difficult task. What has been undertaken here is an account of the most important events which illustrate change and continuity over more than two thousand years. It is not possible to give even treatment to all topics, so choices have had to be made which reflect, apart from the author's interests, the availability of source material. It has been a great pleasure to engross myself in the rich vein of local historical sources which are available for research in the county today. I must also extend my thanks to those who have cast their eyes over parts of the draft—John Aram, Dr. Nicholas Bennett, Neville Birch, Terry Hancock, Michael J. Jones, Dr. Simon Pawley, Stan Warmoth and Neil Wright. Any remaining errors are my responsibility.

1

The Setting

For the purposes of this book Lincolnshire means the historic county and not the modern, smaller administrative unit. The ancient county corresponds to a large distinct region bordered by the North Sea to the east, the Humber estuary to the north, a substantial length of the river Trent to the north-west and an area of Fen to the south. Natural forces exerted over millions of years have resulted in the region of contrasts that can be seen today. The natural environments of Fen, chalk and limestone upland and wide valleys have dictated man's activities in Lincolnshire through the millennia.

The oldest rock beds were formed some 220 million years ago during the Triassic period, which is part of the larger Mesozoic era. During this period of millions of years the first mammals appeared. The small area of Keuper Marls, located in the extreme north-west of the county beneath the Isle of Axholme, dips eastward and is over-laid—first by clays of the Lower Jurassic period, then by limestones of the Middle Jurassic period and further clays of the Upper Jurassic period. The next major deposits occurred after a short period of uplift and gentle tilting during the Cretaceous period. Chalk beds were deposited on top of sands and clays in the Wolds area during a timespan of some 75 million years. For almost the entire Jurassic and Cretaceous periods the region was submerged beneath the sea until the end of the Upper Cretaceous era, 65 million years ago, when it was faulted slightly and uplifted above the sea level.

The present landscape has largely been formed by the effects of climatic changes which alternated between ice ages, the most severe of which covered the entire area under an ice sheet hundreds of metres thick, and warm interglacial periods. In the most dramatic ice age the Anglian ice sheet reached as far south as London. Its retreat revealed how it had scoured the surface, deepening the clay vales and depositing boulder clay which caused the river Trent to change direction from a west-east route, flowing from the Midlands via the Lincoln Gap to the North Sea, to its present course.

1 *Wrawby post mill.*

Nearly two-thirds of the county is under thirty metres above sea level, and a large part of that is less than two or three metres above sea level. The low-lying Fen and coastal plain is mistakenly characterised as

Lincolnshire by many visitors from the industrial towns of the East Midlands on their way to the coastal resorts. Although Lincolnshire contains about one third of the Fen region of England, the rest lies mainly in Norfolk, Cambridgeshire and Huntingdonshire.

There are two hill ranges. In the east, extending from the Humber coast to north of the Fens, the chalk Wolds rise to a height of 151 metres above sea level. To the west of this is the mainly limestone Heath, which begins in the north of the county and follows a line southwards where it broadens and becomes more undulating, reaching a height of 154 metres above sea level. These Kesteven Uplands dip down to the Fens in the east. The western side is characterised be a distinctive escarpment known as the 'cliff' or 'Lincoln edge'. To the west of the cliff is a mainly clay vale through which the river Trent flows to the river Humber and the North Sea.

There are also substantial outcroppings of sands and gravel. In the north west, beyond the river Trent, lies the Isle of Axholme which was largely cut off from the surrounding area until it was drained during the 17th century. Between the Heath and Wolds lies the clay vale through which the river Ancholme flows. This vale, just as the Vale of Trent and the Isle of Axholme, was formed by the actions of Anglian and Devensian glaciations and subsequent flooding. During the post-Devensian warming the sea levels changed from perhaps minus 100 metres to plus eight metres, thus causing the entire Fenland, river Witham valley and river Trent valley to become flooded and leaving Lincolnshire with just 'Wolds' and 'Heath' as islands. This inundation also finally drowned the land bridge which had connected Britain and mainland Europe. Known as the Flandrian transgression, Lincolnshire became covered with large coniferous forests, the evidence of which can still be seen as the remains of tree stumps in the sea at low tide off Huttoft Bank at locations like Anderby Creek and Sutton-on-Sea. The long east coast has been subjected to many changes. The low-lying marshlands to the east of the Wolds comprise two different materials. The Middle Marsh is formed from undulating boulder clay, while the

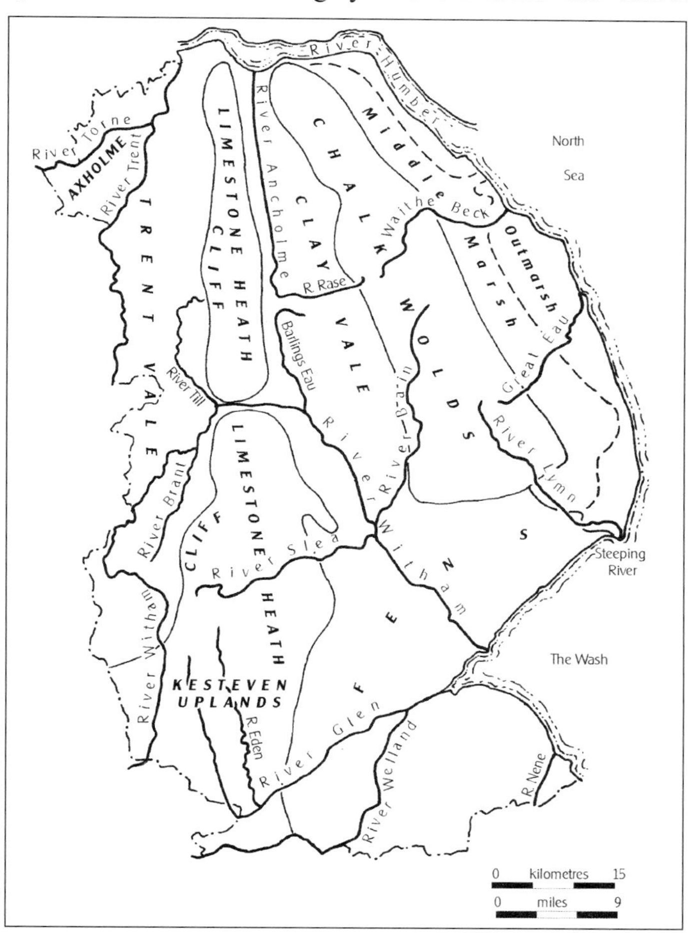

2 *The natural regions of Lincolnshire.*

3 *An 'erratic' deposited at Winceby during glaciation.*

Outmarsh is of much more recent marine silts. This is precarious and is only maintained by the intervention of man with substantial sea defences.

Much of the county remains only a few metres above sea level and river and coastal flooding is prevented only by drainage and sea defence schemes. It is common in Lincolnshire to see fields bordered by drainage dykes and rivers with embankments on each side to protect the surrounding farmland. There is little evidence of the way these rivers once meandered over the wide valley bottoms and low-lying land, forming large areas of marshland. Nor do these tamed rivers give any idea of the former size and power needed to cut wide gaps in the limestone edge. The natural topographical features are the product of millions of years of activity, but over the last millennium man's impact has become more invasive. Towns and villages, connected by road and rail, have been built on some of the most intensively cultivated land to be found anywhere in the world. Despite this, the natural landscape has dictated this activity. The original location of settlements was dependent on the availability of water and good, well-drained land. It is not, therefore, surprising to find relatively few villages in the Fens, or that there are a number of spring-line villages located in a line to the north and south of Lincoln on the west side of the Lincoln Edge. Similarly, throughout the county's history the location of industry has been dependent on natural resources, and of course the routes of roads and, later, railways have been governed by topography and, in particular, drainage.

2

Prehistoric Lincolnshire

4 *Evidence of man's early activity.* (Top) *Flint tools from Kirmington made about 200,000 years ago.* (Middle) *Hand-axe from Roxby made about 60,000 years ago.* (Bottom) *flint arrow-heads from around 11,000 years ago.*

There are great difficulties in establishing the extent of early human activity during the Palaeolithic period. What may be simple worked flints have been discovered in the silt beds beneath the modern surface at Kirmington, but other evidence is so sparse that it is not possible to say whether it represents early activity and, if it does, what kind of activity it was. These flints may have been produced some 200,000 years ago during the warmer interglacial period after the great Anglian ice age. As the climate became warmer early hominids may have wandered over the wide open wastes of Lincolnshire. Hand axes and other artefacts from the lower and middle Palaeolithic periods have been discovered at, for example, Whisby, Roxby, Risby Warren, Barlings and Salmonby, but their rarity has made almost impossible any meaningful reconstruction of the way of life of the tool makers.

During the Devensian period Homo Sapiens first appears. These 'modern' men probably hunted in Lincolnshire, perhaps coming from caves at Creswell Crags on the Nottinghamshire—Derbyshire border, where there is ample evidence of settlement. At this time Lincolnshire was inhospitable, a harsh treeless tundra landscape. However, over a period of time there was a steady rise in temperature which brought with it dense forestation of the entire county, supported by the enriched mineral soil left by glaciation. The land bridge between Britain and mainland Europe allowed the re-colonisation by plant species not reached by the ice sheets. The abundance of vegetation and wildlife allowed man to exist by hunting and gathering. By the end of the Mesolithic period some permanent

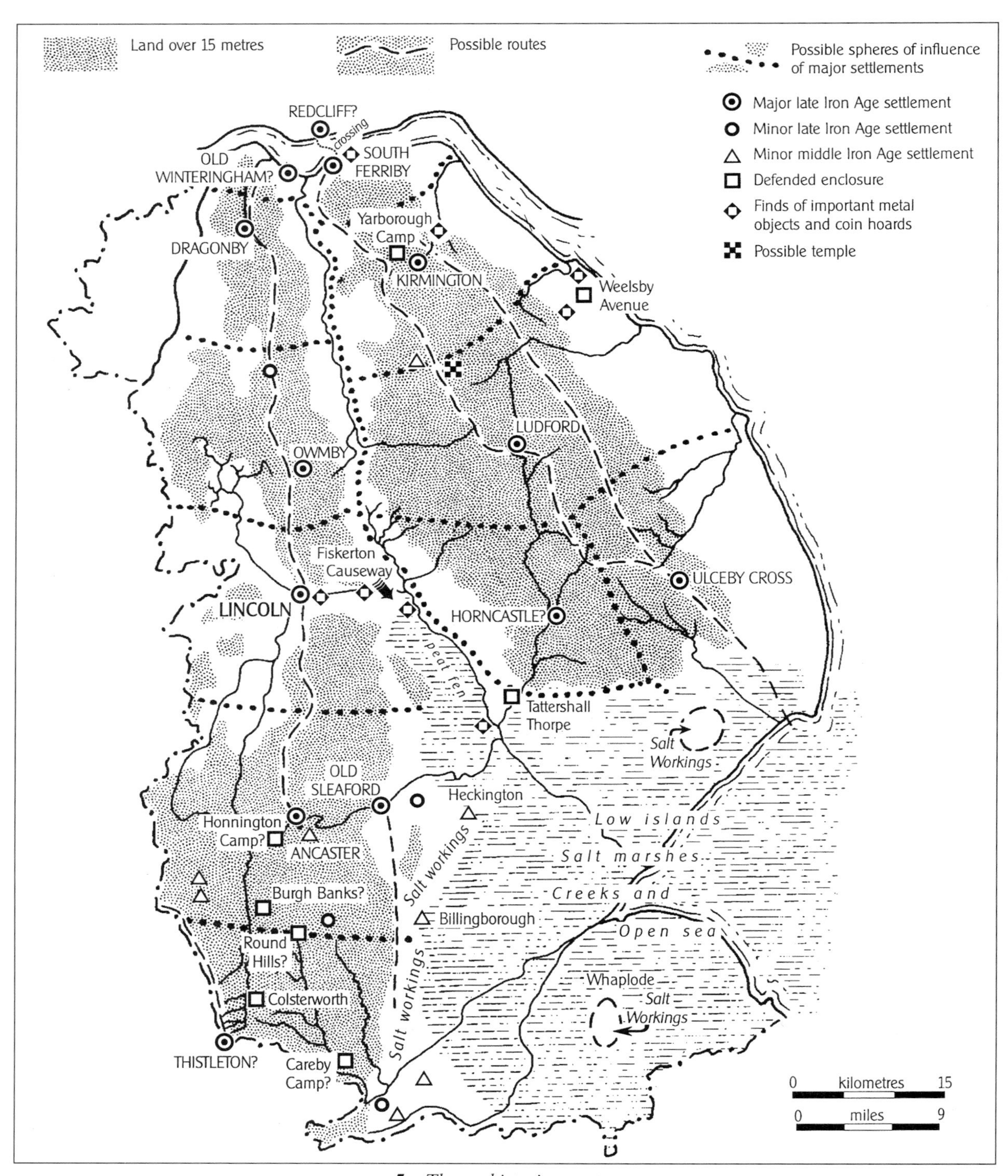

5 *The prehistoric county.*

6 *Bronze-Age axe-head,* c.*2,000 B.C.*

settlements may have been established as areas of forest were cleared to make way for farming, although, as there was an abundance of wildlife, hunting continued to be an important source of food. This new activity can be dated to about 4000 B.C. Farming inevitably required greater sophistication—better tools, better planning, organisation and, perhaps, a more complex social structure. Owing to the time lapse and to destruction by modern farming methods, few sites from this period are known. The earliest so far discovered was at Tattershall Thorpe, where excavation has revealed traces of a wooden building. The evidence of other possible sites is based on finds of pottery and flint artefacts at Dragonby, Little Gonerby and Tallington.

To what extent farming was developed independently in Britain or brought by immigrants is uncertain, despite connections with other areas. Through destruction by modern farming few Neolithic settlements have been identified. Burial sites in the form of earthen long barrows have been found which again, as with pottery, conform to types found throughout northern Europe. These mainly occur on the Wolds where 20 definite and numerous possible sites have been discovered. The best example so far excavated is at Skendleby. Dating from between 3500 and 2700 B.C., it is over 65 metres long and 23 metres wide and contained the complete remains of four people and the partial remains of three others. Barrows provide the most striking example of Neolithic man's activity; flint axe-heads have also been found there and on the uplands north of the river Witham, and, in smaller numbers, on the limestone upland south of Lincoln. Large numbers of axe-heads indicate that forest clearance must have been occurring at an increasing rate, corresponding with a rise in the importance of farming. One aspect of particular interest is the origin of these axes, since local limestone, chalk and sandstone is unsuitable for their construction. Analysis of the stone shows that the majority came from Cumbria, with a significant number from north Wales. Others were found to have originated in Cornwall, Leicestershire, Northumberland, Warwickshire and even as far away as Ireland. This does indicate a level of trade of heavy, bulky items imported to the county despite the lack of wheeled transport.

There is evidence of substantial migration of peoples at the end of the Neolithic period, some 2,500 years before Christ. The Beaker peoples, named after the distinctive pottery they produced, settled widely over eastern and southern England. They can be identified by the different facial skeletal characteristics of a long head shape compared with the round heads of the indigenous population. In Lincolnshire, evidence of Beaker folk has been discovered at a number of sites on the Wolds and around Scunthorpe, Ancaster and Grantham. Pottery provides one source of evidence and barrows provide another. One of the most impressive round barrows in Britain, at over 50 metres diameter, is at Tallington. Round barrows are associated with the later Neolithic period and the Bronze Age and have been found in groups of up to twelve. Despite the number of barrows which have been identified, it probably represents only a small proportion of the total constructed. It is thought that many survived until the 18th century but have subsequently been destroyed by increasingly intensive farming.

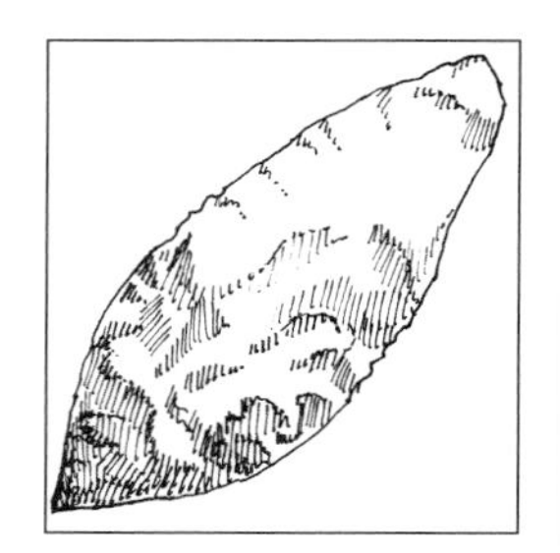

7 *Flint tool.*

By the time of the appearance of bronze metal working in Lincolnshire, the sophistication of flint tools had reached its zenith and they probably remained in use for centuries. The earliest Bronze-Age implement found in the county is an awl from the end of the third millennium B.C. This was followed by examples of daggers, knives, axe-heads, spearheads, and rapiers of different sizes which became more complex in their design. By the later Bronze Age it appears that most settlements were located in river valleys and not, as previously supposed, on higher ground. Over two-thirds of the find-spots of Lincolnshire bronzes lie in the valleys of the river Trent, the river Ancholme, and with a particular concentration on the river Witham at the Witham Gap at Lincoln and eastward to Washingborough.

The Iron Age began about 800 B.C. but iron objects rarely survive from this time. Instead copper alloys, of which bronze is one, remained in common use up to the Middle Ages. As with most technical changes, new technology takes time to develop, and this was true of the quality and quantity of iron production, especially as the quality of bronze also improved over the same period. For this reason, iron objects only became common after the Roman invasion and settlement in the first century A.D.

From halfway through the first millennium BC there was considerable cultural change influenced by the migration of Celtic peoples from Europe. Much is known about the peoples who settled in the East Midlands, not only from archaeological research but, for the first time, from written evidence on coins and in the work of Roman historians such as Cornelius Tacitus who reported extensively on native groups. The new metal work brought by these people was distinctive; it had elaborate abstract interlocking 'S' scrollwork and other normally symmetrical curvilinear designs based on this pattern. Most Celtic art is associated with horsemanship or warfare and was of such quality that they were probably owned by tribal chieftains. Excellent examples have been found in Lincolnshire. The county boasts the Witham Shield, from the Iron Age but constructed from bronze.

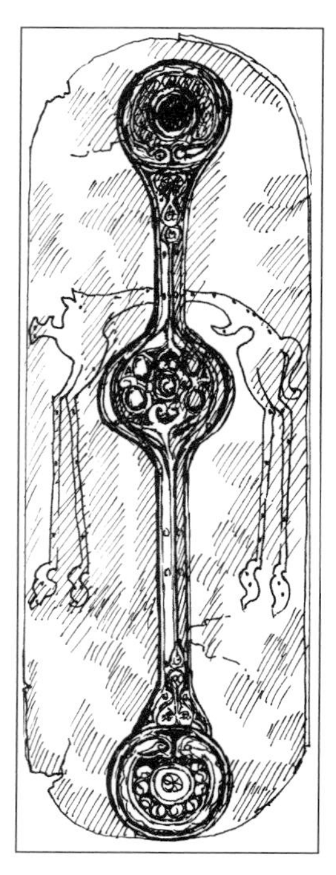

8 *The Witham Shield.*

It is an impressive tribute to the skills of the craftsmen, so much so that it is unlikely to have been used in battle but was probably produced for a symbolic and ceremonial purpose. The original can be seen in the British Museum, but there is an excellent reconstruction which can be seen at the City and County Museum at Lincoln or at other venues throughout the county.

When the Romans came to Britain they found a disunited country composed of a number of loose confederations of tribes. Although they used the disparaging term 'barbarian' to describe these tribes, what they actually found was a society with a well defined social structure of chieftains, aristocrats, priests, tradesmen, craftsmen and peasants, held together with a well developed political, legal, ceremonial and religious system. Lincolnshire was part of the wider area of the Corieltauvi tribe which stretched from the river Humber in the north to the river Nene in the south and included what is now Nottinghamshire and Leicestershire. However, it would appear that the Fens were outside this sphere of influence, because this area had a coastline very different from that of today. It consisted of low islands, salt marshes and open sea subject to enormous tidal differences. The sea had risen over the previous 6,000 years to a point at the beginning of the Iron Age when it began to regress, so that by about A.D. 100 more land was visible than at any time since the land bridge between Britain and mainland Europe had been broken. The coastline may almost have reached Bourne, and then stretched northwards up to South Kyme and then eastwards along the southern edge of the Wolds. When very high tides occurred, the valley of the river Witham as far as Lincoln could have been flooded. Low tides would have revealed large areas of land which, except for a few raised areas, would have been engulfed at high tide. Thus the notion of a defined coastline is not applicable to the Fens. Despite this, extensive work undertaken by the Fenland Project suggests substantial Iron-Age activity, and around one hundred sites have been discovered.

The particular conditions which prevailed in the Fens enabled a salt industry to develop. Salt production began during the Iron Age and carried on throughout the Middle Ages. Production was widespread. The first discoveries were along the beach at Ingoldmells and inland in the parish of Wrangle. Most, however, lay on the Fenland basin edge parishes such as Helpringham, Billingborough to Deeping St Nicholas and Cowbit. These inland areas were particularly suitable. Sea water was trapped in clay beds at high tide after which it evaporated, leaving the salt residue. Sometimes, beds were raised and fires were lit underneath them to speed the process. Salt was widely used and exported to other parts of the country. As well as in the storage of food, it was essential for the preservation of hides. It may have also been used as a medium of exchange.

9 *Iron-Age hut.*

Corieltauvi settlements have been discovered at Kirmington, Ludford, Ulceby Cross and possibly Horncastle on the chalk Wolds; at Dragonby, Owmby, Ancaster on the limestone; and at Old Sleaford on the Fen

10 *Honington Camp.*

edge. They are far enough away from each other possibly to have acted as centres of local administration. Lincoln may not have been a distinct settlement, but perhaps a cluster of settlements close to the river Witham. In addition to village settlements, defended enclosures have also been discovered, although intensive farming has destroyed much of the earthen structures. The best example is Honington Camp which is located close to Ancaster near what is thought to be the Jurassic Way, a route along the Lincoln Edge from the river Humber to Colsterworth. This rectangular enclosure was 150 by 175 metres surrounded by 25-metre wide earth banks and ditches. Other earthen structures have also been discovered at Round Hills near Ingoldsby, Careby Camp near Bourne and, in the north of the county, at Yarborough Camp near Kirmington. The destruction of these sites and the loss of possible dating evidence through deep ploughing means that little is known of their date or function. These were substantial works and must have fulfilled an important function, perhaps as strongholds of local chieftains.

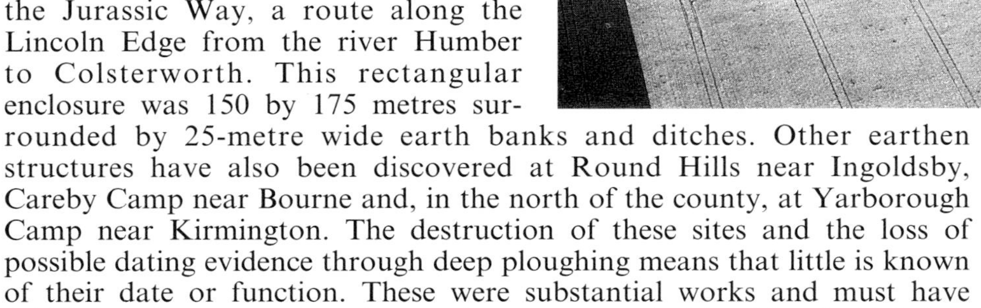

Little is known of the government of this area, though evidence from archaeological artefacts points to highly skilled craftsmen serving a relatively sophisticated society during the period immediately prior to the Roman invasion. For example, bronze jewellery, with complex linking and joints, and beautifully worked gold alloy torcs have been discovered at Ulceby near Kirmington. The high quality of some of these finds in Lincolnshire suggests, along with the swords and shields, that there may have been a wealthy class of noblemen living in the county. There was also likely to have been a merchant class trading with other parts of the county and Europe, and coin pellet moulds found at Old Sleaford would suggest a relatively advanced trading system. Old Sleaford must have been a high order settlement, perhaps some kind of tribal capital; it was certainly on one of the main Iron-Age routes now known as Mareham Lane running in from the south and joining the river Slea. Whether or not the track continued northwards is unknown. In addition to the river network, trade was facilitated by other roads. The Jurassic Way ran from the river Humber, through Lincoln and southwards to the south Midlands. Another track, known now as 'High Street', went from South Ferriby, where there was likely to have been a crossing point of the river Humber, along the western edge of the Wolds; a corresponding track, known as 'Barton Street', ran along the eastern side. Therefore, the Romans found on their entry into Lincolnshire a relatively sophisticated society, and not the 'barbarian' tribe they described.

3

The Romans

Almost a hundred years after the first Roman invasion of Britain in 55 B.C. by Julius Caesar, the Emperor Claudius in A.D. 43 set about conquering the people and subjugating the tribes. Within a few years the Ninth Legion, Legio IX Hispana, had marched northwards and was in Lincolnshire. Their first bases in this area may have been at Longthorne, near Peterborough, Newton on Trent in Nottinghamshire and Great Casterton in Leicestershire, and a further temporary one was possibly established in the Witham gap just to the east of a natural lake, the Brayford Pool. Soon there was a permanent fortification on the hilltop to the north of the gap. The high limestone position provided a dry site that was strategically advantageous, giving a panoramic view over much of the surrounding countryside. To the west were the poorly drained flat lands extending to the river Trent some 15 miles away. Much of this was marsh land interspersed with substantial areas of forest. The river Witham meandered from the south west into the 'Lin' or pool and on through the gap in the limestone ridge before continuing its route south-east into the Fens. The escarpment could be seen stretching northwards with the dip slope descending gently eastwards. The fortification at the top of the hill, established between *c*.A.D. 54 and 60 consisted of a square stockade protected by a square timber box rampart defended by a large V-shaped ditch. Contained within it were rows of wooden barracks, stores and granaries, and at the centre the *principia* or headquarters. The enclosed area would have not been large enough to billet the entire 5,000 or so officers and men who made up the legion, so it is likely that some units were billeted in other parts of the county as the entire area came under Roman control.

11 *Stone relief of a Roman charioteer.*

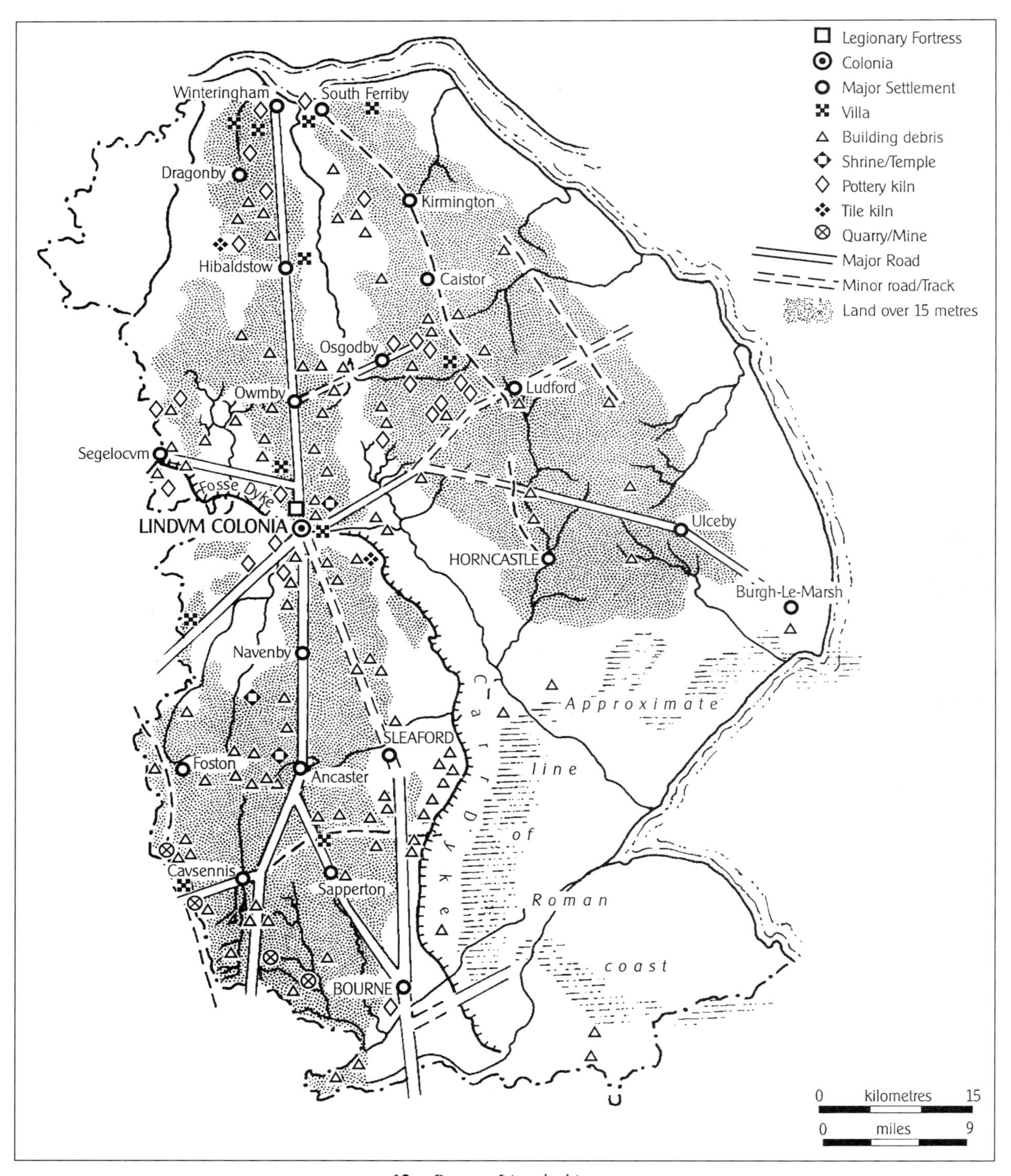

12 *Roman Lincolnshire.*

13 *Roman legionary.*

At the time Lincolnshire could have been classed as the northern frontier of the Roman empire, defined by a zone running in a south westerly line to Bath, Ilchester and Exeter. Some Britons had opposed the Roman advance, but the Corieltauvi appear not to have put up any resistance. Many no doubt gained economically by providing support, trades and services. Although the Corieltauvi seem to have been easily subdued, this was not the same everywhere. In A.D. 60 the IXth Legion, under its commander Petillius Cerialis, was ordered to put down the rebellion by the East Anglian tribe, the Iceni, who, under the leadership of their Queen Boudicca, had sacked undefended Colchester and killed many of the inhabitants. Soon after, the Iceni met the IXth Legion, and by sheer weight of numbers defeated them by killing most of the infantry. This most serious threat to Roman ambitions in Britain only ended when the Iceni were later defeated in the Midlands near Towcester. From then on, the Romans were able to consolidate their control and push the frontier northwards. When the county became relatively settled, the legion was re-deployed northwards beyond the river Humber, and the status of Lincoln was altered from being a garrison town to a *colonia*, a particular classification of settlement catering for retired legionnaires.

Lincoln was the most important settlement in the county, but Roman influence also extended into the countryside. When the army first entered the county, it probably marched along the ancient prehistoric track-ways following the high limestone edge, from Great Casterton, and probably established bases at Ancaster and Navenby. This road, which became Ermine Street, originated in London and was later extended north of Lincoln to Winteringham on the river Humber. The Fosse Way to Bath and Exeter in the south west of the country meant that Lincoln was situated on two of the principal arteries of Roman Britain. Other roads were soon built to facilitate military transport from the subdued south to the new frontier north of the Humber; one passed through Bourne and Sleaford, skirting the Fens, and became known as Mareham Lane. Other roads were built eastwards and westwards which also took advantage of the natural drainage of the uplands. Major roads were built from Lincoln to Ludford and Grainthorpe, and from Lincoln to Ulceby and Burgh-le-Marsh, both terminating at the coast. To the west, Tillbridge Lane branched from Ermine Street to cross the river Trent at Littleborough. The existence of such good roads, though they were built primarily for the military, must have been a boost to the local economy.

These straight roads were for rapid communication, but water transport was normally used for the movement of heavier goods. The construction of two canals, which were on an engineering par with the roads, further stamped the Romans' footprint across the countryside. The 11-mile Fosse Dyke canal, which connected Torksey on the river Trent with the Brayford Pool at Lincoln, and the 56-mile Carr Dyke connecting the river Witham just below Lincoln to the river Nene near Peterborough, opened up the entire county to the transportation of heavy goods. The Carr Dyke also functioned as a catch-water drain and began

the long process of draining the Fens. The river Witham is also likely to have been improved to ensure its navigability from Lincoln to the sea, although the extent of this work is unknown. This internal network of rivers and canals connected with the Midlands via the river Trent and its tributaries and with the military north via the river Ouse to York. Goods could be shipped through the Fosse Dyke, along the river Trent, out of the Humber and along the coast northwards to Hadrian's Wall.

The status of *Lindum* must have been enhanced by its position as a crossing point of rivers, canals and roads. It is not surprising, therefore, that Lincoln's inhabitants enjoyed the fruits of trade from throughout the Empire. For example, fragments of amphorae, which were mostly Spanish in origin and were used to transport wine and other luxuries from the Mediterranean region, have been discovered by archaeologists. In addition, quite large quantities of good quality red Samian ware, often marked with the potter's stamp in the base, produced in Gaul, and German, Italian and Greek marble have been found. The demand for less expensive pottery for everyday domestic use was met from a local industry usually located outside towns. Kilns have been discovered at Dragonby, North Hykeham, Lea near Gainsborough, Market Rasen, South Carlton, Little London, Torksey, and Knaith as well as around Lincoln. Iron was also produced, but on a relatively small scale, to meet the demand for domestic and farming appliances near Scunthorpe and Grantham and, in the south of the county, at Colsterworth, Corby Glen, Ingoldby, Castle Bytham, Wyville with Hungerton, Woolsthorpe and Holywell. The demands for stone for both buildings and defensive walls led to a relatively large-scale quarrying industry. Limestone quarries were to be found at Greetwell (probably serving Lincoln) and Ancaster. The extraction of salt from sea

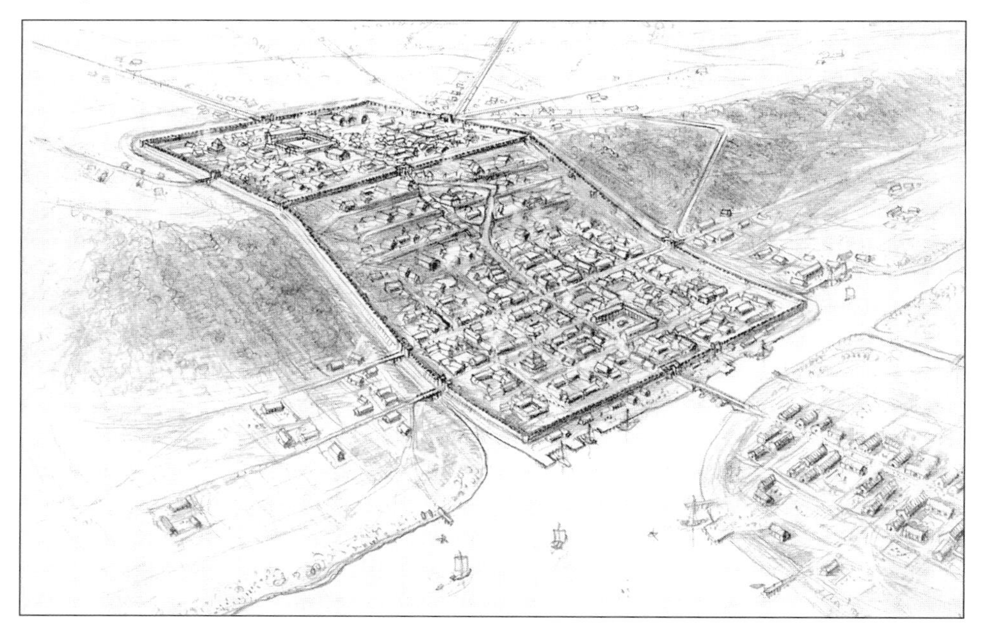

14 Lindum Colonia *in the mid-fourth century.*

15 *The remains of the Newport Arch, Lincoln, once the northern entrance to the city.*

water was also undertaken. Although this industry had earlier origins, it was developed to new levels during the Roman period. Numerous salterns, which used the evaporation method of extraction, have been discovered in the quiet waters of the inner Fens. Salterns have also been discovered at Wrangle, where there was a particularly high concentration, and as far north as Skegness and Ingoldmells. Salt was used extensively to preserve food. Just as specialist commodities such as tin from Cornwall and mill-stone from Derbyshire were imported to the county, salt would have been exported from Lincolnshire.

Without the presence of the Roman army after c.A.D. 78, Lincoln's new status as a *colonia* heralded an era of construction. New ramparts were dug, wooden stockades were replaced by stone walls, and redundant military headquarters became the *basilica* and *forum*, the centre of commercial, religious and civic life. Typically, provincial Roman towns were planned with roads laid out in a grid pattern. Lincoln was no exception. Gates were constructed in each of the four walls. The remains of two—Newport Arch, at the northern side of the city, and East Gate—are still visible today. Evidence at the East Gate shows that the later monumental gate replaced an earlier timber construction of the legionary phase. The West Gate was found in the 19th century at the north-west corner of the castle bank just north of the west gate of the present castle, but it was soon reburied.

By the second century occupation had extended beyond the enclosed hilltop area southwards down the hill to fill in the land north of the river Witham and the hillside was subsequently fortified. The southern gate of this new extended enclosure was on the site now occupied by the Stonebow, which was the main entrance from the Fosse Way and Ermine Street. At this time Lincoln's growing status was shown by its impressive stone walls, monumental gates, public spaces with fountains and statues, public baths and impressive temples. An aqueduct brought water, possibly from a source north-east of the city, which was used in the baths and also to flush out the sewer system. Lincoln became a most impressive town; it was the largest, but not the only, walled town in the county. Caistor, Horncastle and Ancaster had defensive walls but the exact dates of their construction are unknown. The fact that Horncastle has no connecting main road would suggest that the town was walled quite late in the Roman period, although there is some evidence of an early Roman settlement there.

The peaceful nature of the county from the second century A.D. is indicated by the substantial number of Roman dwellings outside the protection provided by walled towns. A large number of villas,

characteristically made of stone with tile roofs and a regular floor plan, was built on the chalk and limestone uplands. One such substantial villa has been discovered at Winterton. This comprised stone buildings on three sides of a square. The living accommodation had painted wall plaster and part of the floor area was heated by a hypocaust system. This building almost certainly supported a mixed farm. Evidence of live-stock and a building for drying grain has been found. Not all villas were on such a lavish scale. One indicator of the wealth of a villa owner is the quality of the mosaic flooring, which ranged from very rudimentary patterns to elaborate designs using the best quality *tessera*. One such large pavement, which was discovered at Horkstow near the river Humber, is now on display at the British Museum. Nothing is known of the surrounding buildings at Horkstow, but the size and quality of the pavement suggest a substantial villa. Villas were not the only buildings to be located in the countryside. Numerous farmsteads, shrines, temples and buildings associated with industrial undertakings, such as pottery making, iron mining, and salt making, have also been found.

The Romans brought with them religious influences which often resulted in a fusion between Roman and Celtic gods. They also introduced a new 'state' religion, more formal and with a centralised authority based in Rome. Despite this official cult, the Romans did not attempt to impose their beliefs and it is likely that the two practices carried on side by side for many years, particularly in less accessible areas. The Romans had many gods and deities. It was common in individual houses to have a shrine to minor gods, and in larger and more affluent dwellings a separate room would be allocated for prayer where small gifts of bread, wine or fruit were left. In Rome, the centre of the Empire, the most elaborate religious rituals and ceremonies were held in the grandest temples. *Lindum colonia*, as an important provincial capital at the outer reaches of the Empire, would have mirrored on a lesser scale events in Rome. There would have almost certainly been more than one classical-style temple, with characteristic imposing columns. There is archaeological evidence of temples, mainly from the remains of altars and inscriptions, but the reconstruction of their actual appearance has to be achieved by studying better preserved examples elsewhere. The change to Christianity occurred in A.D. 313 on the conversion of Constantine I and the new official religion of the Roman Empire spread quickly. A year later Lincoln sent a bishop to the Council of Bishops at Arles in southern France. The most important evidence of early Christianity in Lincoln-shire came from the excavation in the early 1970s of the Victorian church at St Paul-in-the-Bail. There may have been a Christian church on the site by the end of the fourth

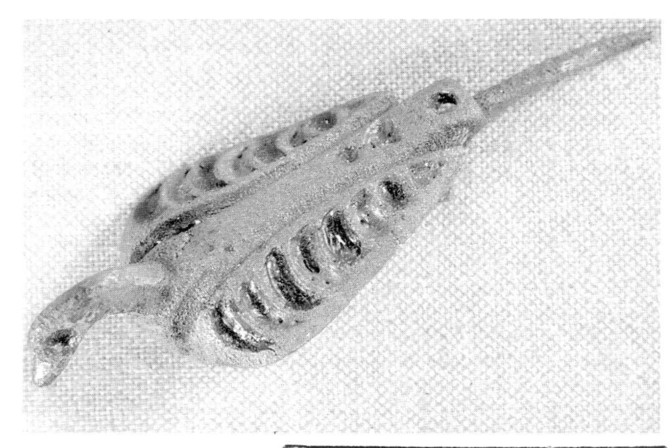

16 *Roman 'Duck' brooch.*

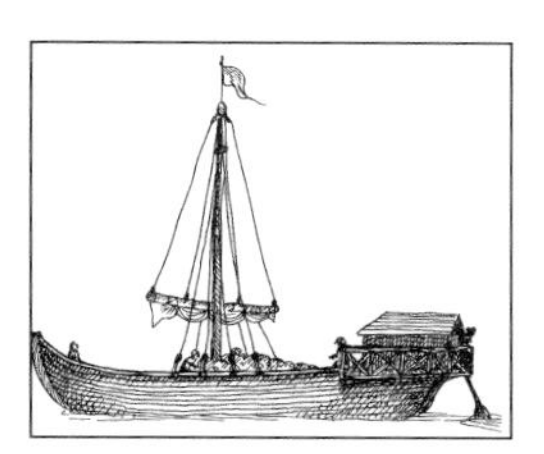

17 *Roman boat.*

century. The fact that this is located in the centre of the Forum shows the status of the new religion. The impact of Christianity on the rest of the county by the end of the Roman period is uncertain although there must have been enclaves in the main centres of population.

By the middle of the fourth century Roman power in Britain was beginning to wane. Throughout the Empire frontiers were coming under attack. In Britain, Hadrian's Wall had been attacked and a number of fortifications were destroyed by the Picts from Scotland in A.D. 343; further attacks were made by the Picts and Scots in 367. At about the same time Saxons from northern Germany were attacking Roman Gaul. It is open to question just how prepared, willing or indeed able the Romans were to protect their Empire, for it appears that some towns and cities in Britain were already in decline. This was not the case in Lincoln, which had been elevated to one of four provincial capitals from *c.*A.D. 300, thus ensuring a measure of prosperity from an influx of government officials. Its new status was reflected in improvements to its fortifications and in the construction of a monumental gate at the lower west entrance of the town. Clearly, such an important town so close to the potentially dangerous east coast was worth defending.

The end of formal Roman control of Britain can be dated to *c.*A.D. 406-410. In 410 Emperor Honorius told the Britons to organise their own defences because this could no longer be undertaken by Rome. The very real fear of attack had already provoked the construction of improved defences at Ancaster, Caistor and Horncastle, as well as improvements to the lower walls at Lincoln. From the middle of the third century the increased vulnerability of the coast had been recognised by the establishment of fortifications, the so-called Saxon Shore, between Portchester on the south coast and Brancaster on the north Norfolk coast. Fortifications may have continued northwards along the Lincolnshire coast but because of coastal erosion all evidence has been lost. One of these forts may have been sited at Skegness, which could have linked with a series of signal stations on the Yorkshire coast. The possible existence of such a fortification is supported by a reference in the 15th-century Court Rolls about neighbouring Ingoldmells, which refers to the existence of a 'castle', and by the construction of a major road to the coast at Burgh-le-Marsh. If this is correct, it is also possible to postulate a second station at the coast near Grainthorpe. It is likely that such a long coast line as that of Lincolnshire would have been defended, particularly as the provincial capital, Lincoln, was so close. By the end of the fourth century these forts may not have been manned by Romans, but by Germanic mercenaries. How many Saxons were already settled in the county by the beginning of the fifth century is not known, but it seems likely that they were already well enough organised to take control once the Romans had departed.

4

Anglo-Saxon and Viking Lincolnshire

It is relatively straightforward to chart the final years of Roman control in Lincolnshire, but far more difficult to say what replaced it. Within a short time, perhaps only a few years, the infra-structure of the Roman imperial system had largely disappeared. After the government and bureaucratic system, designed to maintain Roman laws and levy taxes, came to an end the officials employed to undertake these tasks were redundant. This had a dramatic effect on the trading and artisan classes. Soon the very reason for the existence of towns, as strongholds of Roman government and administration, ceased to be relevant. The trading economy, which had developed and flourished in support of the population, ceased and the economy once again became overwhelmingly agrarian throughout the county. Farming produced little surplus, and thus could not support a large non-agrarian population located in towns. However, towns did not suddenly become deserted, although their populations dramatically declined. Nowhere is this better illustrated than in Lincoln, which very quickly became a shadow of its former glory, with near deserted streets and dilapidated buildings. The walls and monumental gates, once a source of civic pride, soon fell into disrepair—yet survived for several centuries to form the basis of later defences.

18 *A late eighth-/early ninth-century silver hanging bowl found in the river Witham.*

The rate and scale of migration by Angles and Saxons from north Germany is difficult to assess. There is some evidence—from finds of brooches, strap ends and buckles—that Saxon soldiers were in Lincolnshire by the end of the fourth century A.D., perhaps being paid by the Romans as mercenaries to defend the shore. That some Germanic designs were copied and produced locally may suggest that they were here in quite large numbers. This evidence is problematic since such artefacts may only be copied designs rather than an indication of the origin of the wearer. There seems to have been an army, well enough organised and led, to take control of the county on the withdrawal of the Roman army after 410. Certainly the northern Lincolnshire coast was well defended by the end of the fifth century.

19 *Saxons.*

Lincolnshire was never subjected to a uniform invasion. Without Roman control, migration first along the rivers and the Humber estuary would have been quite swift. The migration of peoples across the North Sea would appear to have been relatively peaceful. There is evidence from cemeteries that both Saxon and British burials were taking place during the same period, indicative of both communities living side by side. With the passage of time Anglo-Saxon ritual took over.

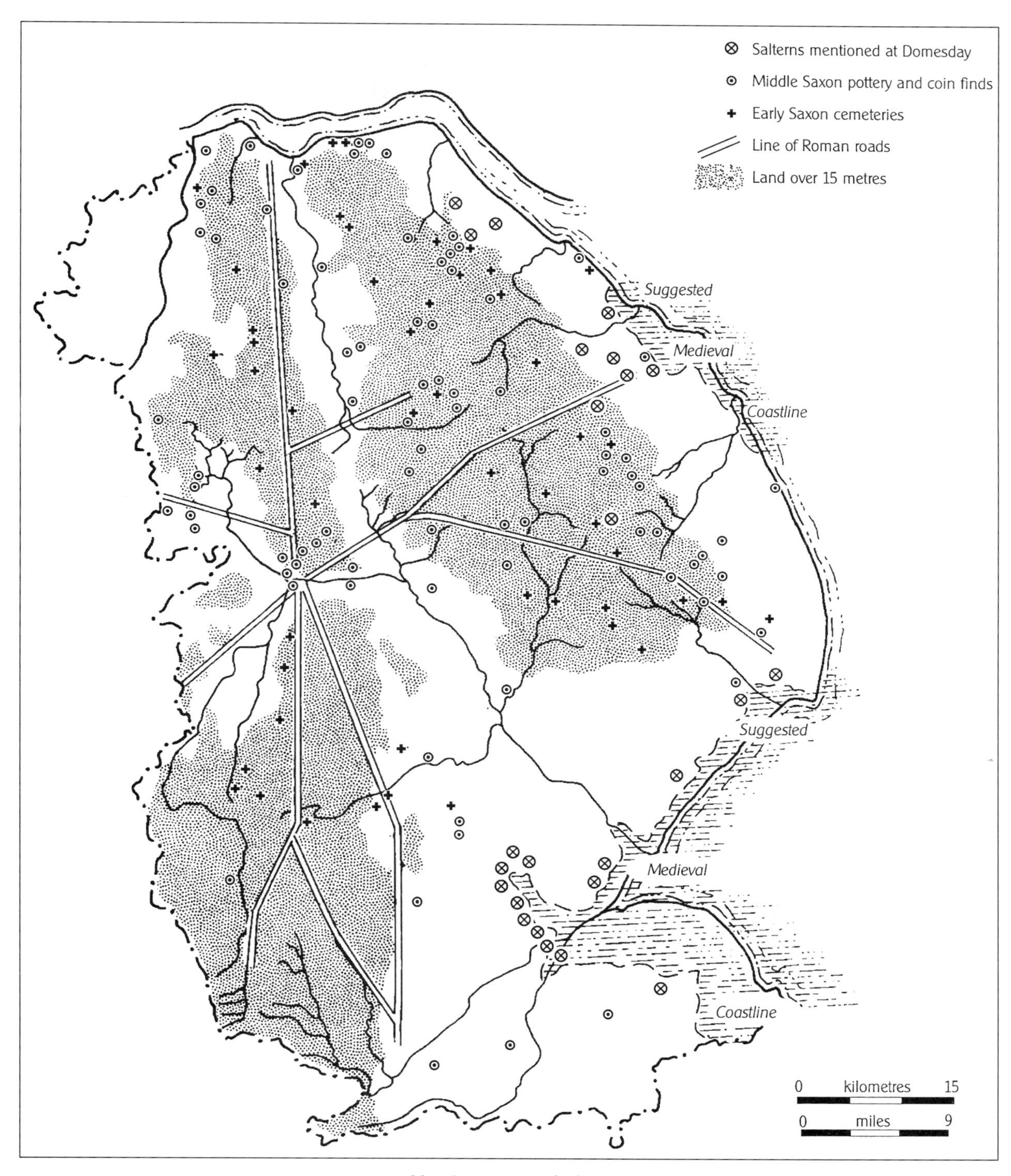

Salterns mentioned at Domesday
Middle Saxon pottery and coin finds
Early Saxon cemeteries
Line of Roman roads
Land over 15 metres
Suggested
Medieval
Coastline
Suggested
Medieval
Coastline
0 kilometres 15
0 miles 9

20 *Saxon Lincolnshire.*

21 *Saxon brooch from Ruskington.*

The northern part of the county was clearly of strategic importance, both because of its coastline and the river Humber estuary, leading traffic into the Midlands from across the North Sea. The county at that time was not unified. Lindsey was a separate kingdom and the area south of Lincoln became part of the central kingdom of Mercia. Geographically, Lindsey was almost an island, lying between the marshland and the sea to the east, the Fen lands and the river Witham reaching nearly to Lincoln in the south, the Humber estuary to the north and the river Trent flood plain to the west. The exact status of Lindsey is a matter of some controversy. However, the case for its being a separate kingdom is strong, perhaps with Lincoln as its capital despite its southern position. Bede's *Historia ecclesiastica gentis Anglorum* in 731 describes Lindsey or *Lindissi* as a *prouincia*, a term usually reserved for a separate kingdom. Bede also mentioned a Bishop of Lincoln called Cyneberht, perhaps a further indication of Lindsey's status. There is also evidence of a royal pedigree of the kings of Lindsey. Lindsey may have been a separate kingdom, but how independent was it? It is certain that the area was fought over by the Northumbrians who wanted to control the river Humber region and to extend their influence further down the coast; and by the Mercians who also wanted to control the Humber to gain access to the sea and the Lindsey coast. The kings of Lindsey seem to have adopted a pragmatic policy of supporting whichever of its more powerful neighbours was in the ascendancy at a particular time. By the eve of the Viking invasion in the ninth century Lindsey had passed under the control of the Mercians.

The numbers of Anglo-Saxons coming to the county during the sixth and seventh centuries is difficult to assess. There were no major concentrations of population, but instead they were spread unevenly throughout the fertile uplands and valleys. Archaeological evidence of Anglo-Saxon activity is limited mainly to finds of coins, pottery and cemeteries. Such evidence as has been found is of settlement on the well-drained chalk and

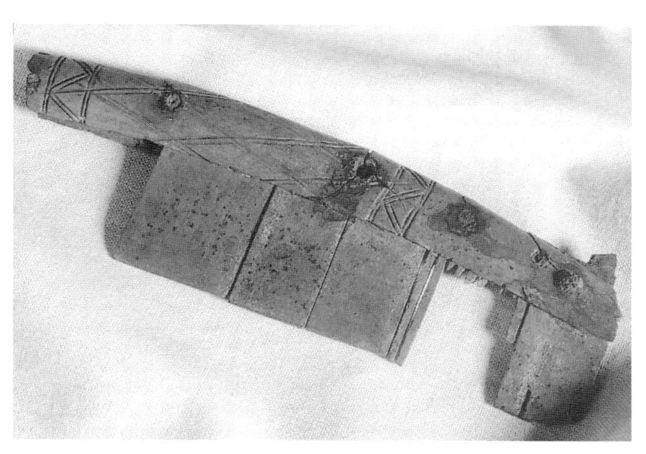

22 *Saxon bone comb (unfinished).*

limestone uplands and, to a lesser extent, on the light sands and gravel around the Fens. None has been found on the heavier soils of the river Trent valley. In addition to archaeological evidence, place names can often identify the origin of settlements; in Lincolnshire there are over 300 with the suffix -ton or -ham denoting Anglo-Saxon origins. These settlements were relatively isolated farming communities producing only enough food for their own consumption. Compared with the sophisticated infrastructure of Roman Britain, the 'Dark Ages' is a term which comes to mind, although recently there has been a reappraisal of the Saxon period which suggests a greater level of sophistication than hitherto thought.

The first Anglo-Saxons were pagan, although there may have been a small Christian enclave in Lincoln, and elsewhere, after the Romans left. Christianity returned more generally to the county again when St Paulinus visited Lincoln and converted Bleacca, the *praefectus* of Lincoln, in the early 620s. During this decade Paulinus had made York his base; he founded a church there, from where to carry out his missionary work. It was at this time he converted the people of Lindsey. These were not isolated events. Paulinus also converted the pagan king of the Northumbrians, Edwin, on his marriage to a Christian Kentish princess at York. Even Mercia, which was ruled by the obstinately pagan king Penda, had become Christian 10 years after his death. By the beginning of the eighth century the impact of Christianity had resulted in the building of religious houses at Crowland, Bardney, Partney, West Halton, Barrow, Hibaldstow and Stow-by-Threekingham and, soon after, at Louth and South Kyme. These religious institutions soon also became centres of learning and administration. The exact status of Lincoln is not clear, although it is likely by this time to have become a principal settlement and home of the kings of Lindsey.

Whilst the movement of the Anglo-Saxons can properly be called a migration, the settlement of the Vikings was, at least initially, a more violent affair. The prospect of rich spoils from the monasteries motivated the first raiding parties. The availability of good farming land and a better climate were longer-term inducements. At home, the growth of tyrannical royal power, changes in land tenure and a growing population may all have contributed to the increased emigration. The Vikings had ships suitable to cross the North Sea and manoeuvrable enough, with a shallow draft, to navigate rivers. Britain was not their only destination for they were migrating into northern Russia and down the European coast to northern France. The first attack on the English shore, recorded in the *Anglo-Saxon Chronicle*, was at Holy Island in 793. Sporadic raids continued, but the most concerted attacks took place in the middle of the

I *The remains of Castle Bytham.*

II *The Roman Ermine Street, north of Ancaster.*

III *Farming on the fens around Donington.*

ninth century. Lincolnshire was first attacked in 841. Little is known about these early encounters. What the *Chronicle* describes as 'a great heathen army' landed in 865 in East Anglia and over the next 15 years took control of most of the eastern part of England including what had been Mercian Lincolnshire. Also in this period the Bishop of Leicester was forced to move southwards, to Dorchester-on-Thames, for protection from Viking aggression. The great army must have traversed the county a number of times, but wintered at Torksey in 872-3, and must have caused havoc as farms on their route and around Torksey were plundered. Further waves of Vikings began to settle, perhaps in the first instance just for the summer months. Settlements developed along navigable rivers and the farmed land committed the newcomers to stay. As with the Anglo-Saxons, it is difficult to assess the impact on the area of these settlers. Archaeological evidence of settlement is scarce. Goltho, in the clay vale east of Lincoln, provides the best evidence, although it is untypical of a Viking settlement. Research has indicated that a fortified earthwork enclosure superseded an earlier Saxon settlement. The fortification consisted of a six-metre wide rampart, on which was constructed a timber palisade surrounded by a 2½-metre deep ditch. Inside the enclosure were a fine hall, kitchen and weaving sheds.

Place names provide some idea of the extent and general distribution of settlements. According to the Domesday Survey, Lincolnshire contains approximately 218 place names ending with 'by' which denotes anything from a farmstead to a village; the far less common 'thorpe' which indicates settlements usually located on more marginal land; and 'holm' connected with low-lying land near a river or lake. This last classification is likely to be associated with a later phase of migration when more fertile land had already been settled. On arrival the Vikings would not have found virgin land, but a county in which the most fertile land was already cultivated. Being powerful aggressors, they may have thrown the Saxons off their land and redistributed it among their followers. In such circumstances settlements could have been renamed. However, it also seems likely that they established separate settlements because so many Saxon place names remain. There is a particular concentration of early Viking settlements on the southern Wolds, with a thinner distribution over the rest of the Wolds, along the river Trent Valley and the Kesteven uplands. For the majority of Saxons remaining in Lincolnshire the only thing that changed was the person to whom they paid their taxes.

23 *Stamford Ware jug.*

Politically, changes also occurred. By 878 the Vikings had driven the Saxon King Alfred into the West Country, where he was able to regroup his forces and defeat the Danish King Guthrum at the Battle of Edington. As a result, in 886 the Treaty of Wedmore established the political boundary between Saxon Wessex, Saxon Mercia and the Danelaw, an area including Lincolnshire where Danish customs prevailed. Beyond the river Humber lay the Danish Kingdom of York which had been overrun in the early 10th century. The English under King Edward

24 *St Peter's Church at Barton-on-Humber has 10th-century origins.*

the Elder, son of Alfred the Great, had by 917 captured East Anglia as far as the river Welland and then marched northwards to Stamford where they took control of Kesteven. At the same time Nottingham, Leicester and Derby were falling to English control and in 918 Edward was recognised as King of Mercia. Lindsey at this time was under the control of Danish York until its destruction in 926 by Edward's successor, Athelstan. He became the first Saxon ruler since Offa of Mercia, a century and a half earlier, to hold complete control of central, northern, and southern England including all of Lincolnshire, proclaiming himself 'King of all Britain'. The political unity of the English kingdom is suggested by the coinage. A mint probably existed at Lincoln as early as the 920s, although by about 973 King Edgar was having coins struck to a unified design at Lincoln and Stamford as well as at other towns in the country. Soon after this, coins were being struck at Caistor, Grantham, Horncastle and Torksey, but these mints were short-lived, surviving only until about 980.

By 942, according to the *Chronicle*, Lincoln, Stamford, Nottingham, Leicester and Derby were given special Borough status. The exact function of these Boroughs is uncertain, but they have in common either a position on a navigable river, or a Roman or prehistoric route-way. One possible explanation is for trade and, of the 'Five Boroughs', Lincoln provides the best evidence. By the early 10th century Lincoln was seeing renewed economic expansion. Archaeological research shows the establishment of new streets and buildings within the old lower southern Roman enclosure, as well as substantial riverside activity and land reclamation. Trade with northern and western Europe was taking place, though the impact of such trade on Lincolnshire would appear to have been relatively small. Evidence from the contemporary Coppergate site at York found that 500 out of 15,000 objects had been imported. It is not possible to make a direct comparison between Lincoln and York because York remained in the Scandinavian sphere of influence whereas Lincoln was in the English sphere. Like York, Lincoln was accessible by river from the North Sea, although the route may not have been continuously navigable. Traded goods could be carried along the river Witham to the inland 'port' on the Brayford, before being trans-shipped along the Fosse Dyke to the Midlands. Once again there is a question mark over its continuous navigability; it is likely that it would have been periodically silted up. The principal items

imported from Scandinavia were walrus ivory, soapstone and the mineral schist. Quernstones were imported from Germany and there is evidence of Scandinavian traders acting as middlemen, since fragments of silk have been discovered. Domestic trade was on a far greater scale. Inevitably, most important were perishable agricultural goods of which little direct evidence remains. This is not the case with pottery, almost indestructible, and most archaeological excavations produce large amounts of it. Pottery was widely produced for the local market, but in some centres its production was on a large standardised scale. Production methods had developed. Wheel-thrown pottery was being produced in contrast to the often crude hand-made ware of the Anglo-Saxon period. Two important centres developed from the middle of the ninth century at Lincoln and Stamford producing a wide range of pottery including cooking vessels, table-ware, lamps and crucibles. The best evidence of pottery production at Lincoln is provided by the kilns, which were excavated in 1973 in Silver Street, an area of development during the Viking period. At Stamford some kilns were located just outside the walls. Wares from both kilns were traded widely and have been found throughout Lincolnshire and the Midlands. Stamford ware has been discovered as far north as Aberdeen and Perth and a complete jar produced at Lincoln has been found in a grave at Birka in Sweden.

25 *The Saxon church of St Mary at Stow was founded in 975.*

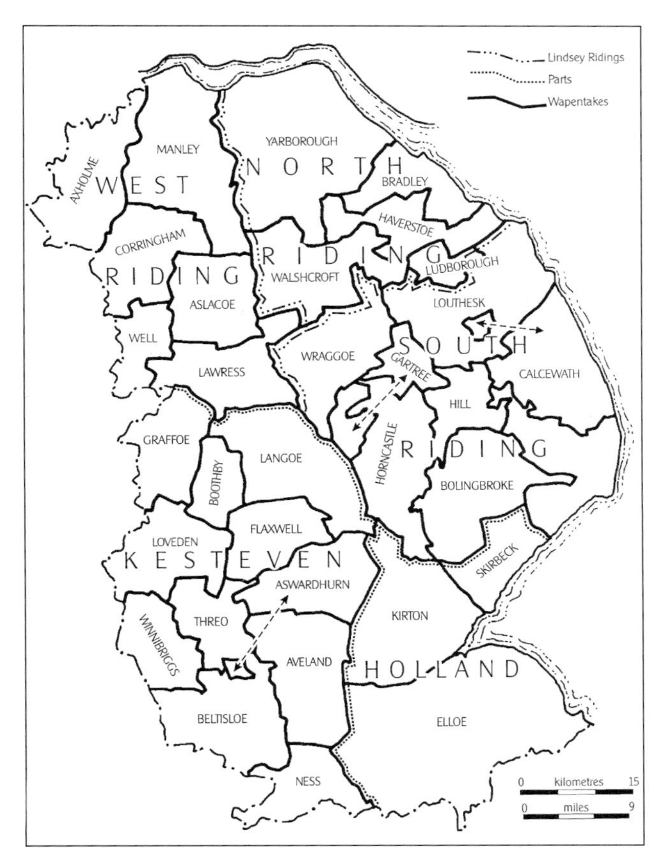

26 *The beginning of formal administration of Lincolnshire in the 10th century.*

During the last decade of the first millennium the Danes again turned their eyes to England, this time by launching sporadic raids along the east and south coasts. The Lindsey coast was almost certainly attacked at this time. Their aim was to extort 'Danegeld': protection money from the English. Substantial sums were involved, rising from £10,000 in 991 to a little less than £90,000 in 1018. In 1013 the Danish King, Swein Forkbeard, occupied Lindsey so that he could launch an attack southwards. From here he executed a successful campaign when he forced the English king, Athelread 'The Unready', to seek safety in Normandy. Swein did not live long enough to enjoy his victory; he died at Gainsborough in 1014, when he was succeeded by Cnut. By this time the English forces had regrouped and were marching north towards his Lindsey base. Cnut was unready and fled to Denmark leaving his Lindsey supporters to feel the full brunt of Athelread's revenge. According to the *Chronicle*, Lindsey 'was ravaged and burnt, and all the men who could be got were killed'. However, the following year Cnut returned to England and this time successfully became King of the English, thereby uniting for a short period the thrones of England and Denmark.

During the early part of the 10th century Lincolnshire started to become a distinct administrative unit with a separate shire court held at Lincoln. The position of Stamford at this time is interesting since it was the only one of the 'Five Boroughs' not to become a county town. Apparently by the beginning of the 10th century it was of some importance occupying a strategic site crossing the river Welland. By this time a fortress had been constructed, but this probably did not make it important enough ever to have been considered the county town of potential 'Stamfordshire'. Probably because of its central position on the southern border of Lindsey, Lincoln became the county town. By the end of the century much of the structure of local government was in place. Because of its size, Lincolnshire was sub-divided into Kesteven, Holland and Lindsey. Lindsey was further sub-divided into three 'ridings', each with its own court. However, most day-to-day government was exercised in 33 wapentakes, which remained as a basic unit of administration until the middle of the 19th century.

5

The Impact of the Normans

Almost a thousand years after the Romans built their first fortresses, the county began a new phase of dramatic change brought about by William, Duke of Normandy's invasion in 1066 and what is arguably the most famous event in English history: The Battle of Hastings. Crowned king of England on Christmas Day at Westminster Abbey, William, for the first four years of his reign, was in an uncertain position and he became involved in a number of campaigns throughout England and Wales to subdue dissident factions. One such campaign was in the summer of 1068 when he was forced to put down a rebellion in Yorkshire. On William's return to London his army travelled through Lincolnshire ordering castles to be built, at Lincoln to control the north of the county, and later at Stamford to control the south. That Stamford was the only non-county town in which William ordered the building of a castle supports its possible status as the county town of south Lincolnshire. Both towns had in common the fact that they were located on important routes, and were thus strategically important. At this time the Roman Ermine Street would still have been the principal route down the east of the country from York. As well as these Lincolnshire castles others were built—on William's journey to York at Warwick, Nottingham and York and on his return to London at Huntingdon and Cambridge. The building of these castles may have had a subduing effect on the people of the county, and on the whole the inhabitants seemed to accept their new masters. The county, however, was not unaffected by hostility towards the Normans. In 1069 Edgar the Atheling, who had been widely supported by the English on the death of King Harold at the Battle of Hastings, returned to York from Scotland where he had taken flight. Edgar was also supported by men from a 240-ship Danish fleet, which had sailed up the Humber. Using York as his base, he began to plunder Lindsey but was forced to flee to the Isle of Axholme with a few supporters after being attacked by what must have been a substantial garrison from Lincoln. Yorkshire was

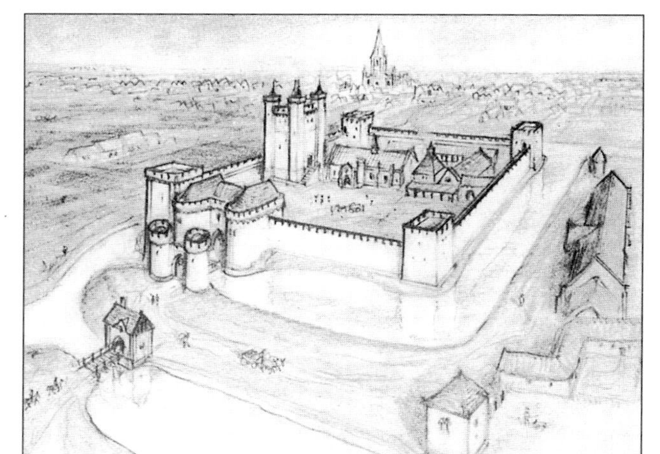

27 *Sleaford Castle.*

28 *Lincoln diocese.*

prepared to support these attempted Danish rebellions and was severely dealt with by King William. Perhaps to maintain the support of the people of Lincolnshire, William held hostage in Lincoln castle some of the most important inhabitants. In 1070 the Swedish King Swein himself entered the Humber in what was to be the last, if short-lived, attempt to return England to the Danish empire, for William soon made a peace. Some rebels, however, led by Hereward, a thegn from Bourne, went to the south of the county, attacking and burning Peterborough and then taking refuge in the Isle of Ely. William attacked them and killed most of Hereward's supporters although Hereward escaped to enter the realms of legend. Lincolnshire, despite these first few years of uncertainty for William, for the most part was not identified with rebellion. Yet the county was substantially affected by the conquest. Firstly, there was the subjugation of the population by military force, by building castles; secondly, the relocation of a cathedral at Lincoln and the installation of the Norman Bishop Remigius; and thirdly the changes in administration, land control and taxation which is illustrated in the great survey, Domesday Book, carried out in 1086, just two years before William's death.

The presence of castles had both the desired oppressive effect on the local population and also provided the centre from which local government and law could be exercised. Castles were also places at which knights could fulfil their military obligations or the obligations of their lord, and were centres of the estates where the king and lords could administer their often far-flung lands. In all cases they were places of administrative activity. The concept of royal government was a Norman import. Whereas the Saxons, prior to the Conquest, had relied on a more subtle system of royal courts dispensing the decision of a central government, Norman castles were built as a visible symbol of power, to demand and maintain William's authority as king.

The choice of Lincoln is not surprising. At the time of the Conquest it was one of the largest and most prosperous towns in the country with a population of approximately 6,500 in 970 dwellings, and was a thriving commercial centre. Lincoln castle was a typical Norman castle following a motte-and-bailey pattern of construction. Strategic considerations required the castle to be built quickly and it is recorded in Domesday Book that 166 dwellings were destroyed to make way for

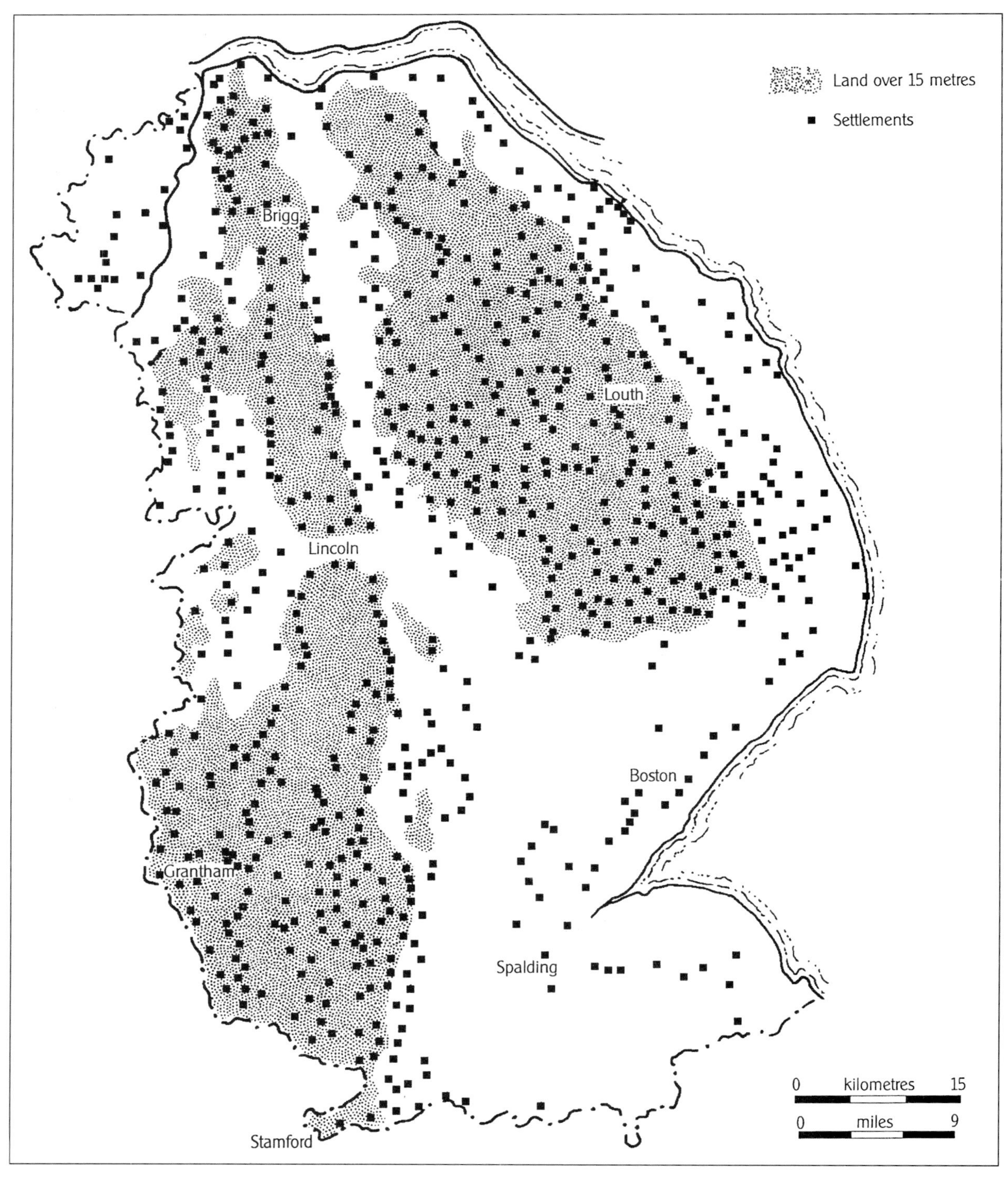

29 *Settlements in Lincolnshire in 1086.*

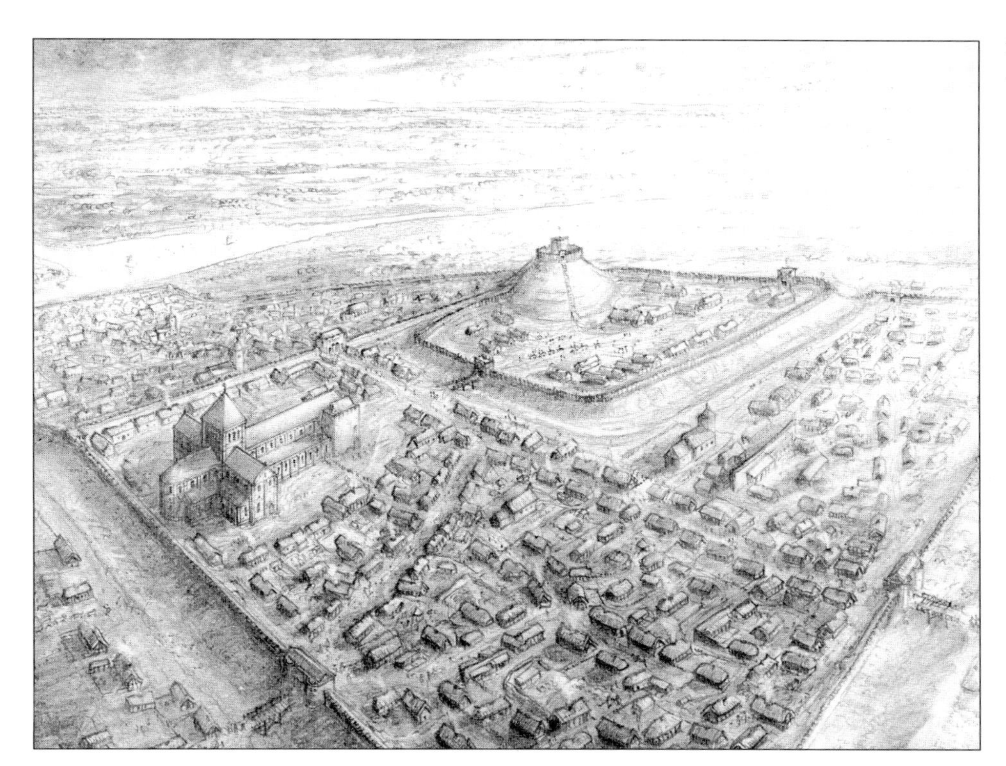

30 *Lincoln in the early 12th century.*

the 13-acre site. Recent research suggests that, because of William's insecure position, a motte (now known as Lucy Tower) 14 metres high was constructed on the ridge overlooking the river Witham valley, making use of the upper enclosure of the Roman town as a bailey. Soon afterwards new ditches and ramparts were dug to form an inner bailey. On top of the motte was constructed a wooden keep. The bailey ramparts were also initially topped with wooden fences. There were probably two wooden gateways with wooden bridges on the sites of the present gates. Wooden defences were quick to build and allowed time for the banks to settle before heavier stone walls and gateways could be constructed. Stamford castle was also begun in 1068, a motte and bailey built initially with wooden fences. For major strategic castles like Lincoln and Stamford, wood could only be a temporary measure; its inherent weakness was that it could easily be set on fire, as graphically illustrated in the Bayeux Tapestry.

The first strategically sited castles were important for subduing any possible revolts and were built on William's orders; other castles were built by tenants-in-chief. These could also be of strategic importance as at Gainsborough and Owston on the river Trent. As the king became more secure and the threat of revolt receded, Lincoln castle became the centre of local government. By 1086, a shire-reeve or sheriff had been installed there, responsible for implementing royal laws and collecting taxes throughout the entire county. In other parts of the county castles

were built to administer the substantial estates created by William and to receive their honorial entitlement. The first such castle was probably built at Castle Bytham by 1086 as the centre of the estates of Drew de Beurere, the lord of Holderness, in Lincolnshire. Later, Bishop Alexander (the Magnificent), who was responsible for rebuilding the cathedral after it was destroyed by fire in 1141, also had castles built at Sleaford and Newark. Most of Lincolnshire's 32 castles were built during the first century after the Conquest.

The building and manning of these castles immediately after the Conquest had the effect of subjugating the population; the building of the great cathedrals brought about a more spiritual control. The new age of religious expression was, like castles, imported from Normandy and took on a new zeal under Pope Gregory VII after 1073. The relationship between William and the church was already close and William had gained papal consent for his invasion. He was also supported by leading clerics. Bishop Odo of Bayeux (who was later responsible for commissioning the Bayeux Tapestry) was William's half-brother and took an active part in the invasion. Remigius, the almoner of the abbey of Fécamp who became Bishop of Dorchester in 1067, was rewarded with substantial lands and the largest diocese in England for providing a ship and 20 knights for the invasion force after the timely death (for William) of the English bishop, Wulfwig. The major see at Canterbury remained in the hands of the Saxon bishop Stigand until 1070, when after a quarrel with William and on papal authority he was deposed and replaced by the king's loyal friend, Lanfranc.

At the time of the Conquest the bishop's seat was not at Lincoln but at Dorchester-on-Thames. There has been some uncertainty as to whether Lindsey can be counted as part of the enormous diocese. York had been Paulinus' base for the conversion to Christianity of the peoples of north Lincolnshire and, therefore, Lindsey was claimed to be within York's sphere of authority, despite the fact, that as early as 1061, Pope Nicholas II had issued a Bull awarding the disputed territory to the diocese of Dorchester. The matter was finally settled in 1092, just in time for the consecration of the new cathedral, when Lindsey was finally placed with Lincoln. The result was an enormous diocese extending from the south bank of the river Humber in the north, through the midland counties (the Saxon kingdom of Mercia) to the river Thames in the south, making it the largest in the country. Remigius began to build his new cathedral at Dorchester but stopped when, in 1072, the Council of Windsor decreed the 'episcopal' sees should be located in larger towns. On the face of it

31 *Lincoln Cathedral in 1092.*

Lincoln would appear to have been an unlikely location over places like Leicester because it was not in a central position. The choice of Lincoln was probably for political reasons; by placing the bishop's seat at Lincoln, Remigius had greater claim to the disputed area of Lindsey. In addition, William's position was still uncertain and York had been associated with rebellion. Thus the concentration of religious and military power just south of the river Humber made strategic sense. In the beginning the cathedral probably had a military as well as a religious function. Its solid Romanesque arches, with built-in machicolations so that stones and other missiles could be dropped on attackers, and arrow loops along the west front, made it a formidable fortress. The establishment of the diocese enabled the episcopal structure to develop. Early in his reign, William ordered that separate courts should be set up for the clergy. The diocese of Lincoln was thus divided into seven archdeaconries, roughly coinciding with the counties covered by the diocese. A little later, Lincolnshire was divided into two; the archdeaconry of Stow, where there was already a pre-Conquest church, which covered the northern half of the county, and the archdeaconry of Lincoln, covering the rest of the county.

At the Christmas Council of 1085 William ordered a survey to establish the ownership of every property throughout the kingdom. The *Saxon Chronicle* states,

> ... the King had deep speech with his counsellors ... and sent men all over England to each shire ... to find out ... What or how much each landholder held ... in land and livestock, and what it is worth ...

In some respects such an enormous undertaking as Domesday Book reflects the insecurity of William, since behind it was a need to assess both the strength and resources of the realm, and the individual wealth of his tenants-in-chief to determine his entitlement to military service. The fact that it was completed, however, suggests that there was a relatively high level of order and central control. The Lincolnshire section of the survey is particularly thorough, perhaps reflecting the economic importance of the county. It includes approximately 2,300 entries relating to 790 settlements. Not only does Domesday Book give information about the control of land, it provides data about the type of land—arable, pasture, meadow, woods or waste; the different classes of inhabitants; whether there were mills, salt-houses, sometimes fisheries and if the village contained a church and a priest. Finally it provides a valuation of the village at the time of the Conquest and at the time of the survey. The distribution of these settlements is very similar to the distribution of modern ones, which had been established by Saxon and Viking settlers. The rural population consisted principally of sokemen (10,851), villagers (7,034) and smallholders (3,317). These figures represent the heads of households. Lincolnshire has a high proportion of sokemen compared with many other counties, possibly because they were the descendants of the Scandinavian armies who had established themselves in the county during the ninth century. Consequently, they

were relatively free and with the villagers were the owners of the plough teams described in the Domesday Survey. Smallholders, on the other hand, were less free and were paid as labourers on the lord's demesne, having little or no land of their own.

The survey makes clear how much the control of land had changed since the Conquest. Under the feudal system, William owned all lands and gave it to tenants-in-chief in return for a military service known as 'knights fee'—the provision of a set number of knights to undertake service for the king. In return for this service they were entitled to the receipt of tithes and rents and various forms of day labour from the inhabitants of the village. The greatest change, although it was not immediate, was felt by the defeated Anglo-Saxon and Anglo-Danish thegns. Initially, William had been content to rule by using the existing landholding hierarchy. However, after attempted rebellions in the north, it soon became apparent that this would not be possible. For example, Morcar, Earl of Northumberland, who had been Harold's sheriff in Lincolnshire, submitted to William only to leave his court and take up arms against him; he was consequently dispossessed of his land at Kirkby le Thorpe, Evedon, Ewerby Thorpe, Howell, Heckington and Quarrington which formed one manor. South Kyme, Boothby Graffoe, Wellingore, and Bassingham (which included Thorpe-on-the-Hill) were transferred directly to the king. William also had the great manor of Grantham. Within Grantham's jurisdiction were Gonerby, Harlaxton, North and South Stoke, Great Ponton, Old Somerby, Sapperton, Braceby, Welby, Belton, Harrowby, Dunsthorpe, Londonthorpe, Barkston, Denton and Skillington. King William also held the manor of Kirton-in-Lindsey which included under its jurisdiction Glentworth, Hemswell, Harpswell, Snitterby, Saxby, Greyingham, Corringham, Aisby, Heapham, Springthorpe, Morton, Somerby, Blyton, Pilham, Northorpe, Ashby, Hibaldstow, Stainton, Redbourn, Brumby, Bottesford, Yaddlethorpe, Winterton and Scunthorpe. There were some 90 tenants-in-chief in Lincolnshire, but they were by no means equal. All were Normans, except for Kolsveinn, who did not own land at the time of the Conquest but by 1086 had been given substantial lands in a number of villages just north of Lincoln and in central Kesteven, in Lincoln itself and some outlying lands in north and eastern Lindsey. What he had done to ingratiate himself with William is unknown. All the new chief tenants were certainly supporters and a number were relations. Count Alan, who was granted enormous tracts of land in the Parts of Holland, was William's uncle; Bishop Odo of Bayeux, who acquired land in over 80 villages and the town of Grimsby, in addition to vast estates in other parts of the country, making him one of the most powerful men in England, was William's half-brother. Others, such as Gilbert of Ghent, had interests in approximately 110 villages, Earl Hugh of Chester in 74, and the Bishop of Lincoln in 58 villages. The tenure of land described in Domesday Book is very complicated. The table overleaf shows the land held in Lincolnshire from the king by Bishop Odo of Bayeux:

Village	Arable land held by Bishop Odo (Plough land)	Principal tenant(s) of the Bishop (Plough land)	Other tenants (Plough land)
S Carlton	1.5		
Ingleby	4	Kolsveinn and Wadard (4)	
Sturton by Stow		Ilbert (4)	16 villagers (4)
Willingham by Stow		Ilbert (1)	2 villagers, 3 sokemen (1)
Ingham		Ilbert (2)	2 villagers, 3 smallholders, 3 sokemen (1)
Coates (part of Ingham)	0.5	Ilbert	has 3 villagers, 2 smallholders (1)
Glentworth		Wadard (0.5)	6 sokemen, 1 villagers (0.5)
Hemswell		Losoard	has 2 villagers, 2 smallholders (1)
Glentham		Wadard (1)	2 villagers, 1 sokeman (1)
Normanby by Spital		Ilbert	has 2 sokemen (1)
Firsby		Ilbert (2)	8 villagers, 8 smallholders, 6 sokemen (2)
Toft by Newton		Ilbert	has 5 sokemen (1.5)
Northorpe		Ilbert (1)	5 villagers, 3 smallholders (1)
Cleathem		Ilbert (1)	3 villagers, 2 smallholders (1)
Stainton & Waddingham		Ilbert (1)	6 villagers, 2 smallholders (1)
Elsham		Ilbert	has 6 villagers, 1 bordar (1)
Audleby	3		15 villagers, 3 sokemen, 6 smallholders (2) + 2 ploughing oxen
Newton	3		
Sumerlede	1.5		8 sokemen (1)
Risby	2		14 sokemen, 4 villagers (3)
Kingerby	2		8 sokemen (1)
Osgodby	land for 10 oxen		9 sokemen (1) + 2 ploughing oxen
Nettleton		Erneis and Wadard (2)	13 villagers, 5 smallholders (1) + 2 oxen
N Thoresby & Audby	2 bovates		
Rothwell	1 bovate		1 sokeman with 1 ox
Grasby	2		6 villagers, 6 smallholders, 11 sokemen (2)
Swallow	2		8 sokemen (1)
Keelby		Wadard (1)	2 villagers, 3 sokemen 2 oxen
Stallingborough			8 villagers, 2 sokemen (1)
Healing		Wadard (1)	3 villagers, 5 smallholders, 2 sokemen (1)
Thrunscoe	0.5		1 villein, 3 sokemen (0.5)
South Coates			16 sokemen (3)
Great Coates			2 sokemen 2 ploughing oxen
Itterby		Ilbert	5 sokemen, 2 villagers (1.5)
West Rasen		Wigmund (1)	7 villagers, 3 smallholders (1)
Middle Rasen		Wadard	has 18 villagers, 11 smallholders (5)
Toft near Newton		Wadard (1)	3 villagers, 11 sokemen (5)
Tealby		Losoard (1)	3 villagers with 3 oxen
N Thorsby & Audby		Ilbert (2)	23 villagers, 5 sokemen (2) + 5 oxen
			27 sokemen (5) less 2 oxen
Great Sturton		Ilbert (1)	3 villagers, 3 smallholders, 23 sokemen (4)
Ranby	1		3 villagers, 1 bordar, 4 sokemen (1)
Burreth			1 villagers, 1 bordar 1 ploughing ox
Hainton		Ilbert (0.5)	9 villagers, 2 smallholders, 1 sokeman (2)
Southrey			2 villagers (0.5)
Strubby			3 sokemen (0.5)
Barkwith			3 sokemen (0.5)
Sotby		Ralph	has 16 sokemen, 3 villagers (4)
Langton		A bishops man ? (1)	26 villagers, 3 sokemen have 5 ploughing oxen
Thimbleby			5 villagers, 3 sokemen (2)
S Willingham		Wadard (1)	4 villagers, 1 *bordar (1)*
Kirkby on Bain		Ilbert (1)	10 villagers, 4 smallholders (1)
Sixhills		Ilbert (1)	3 villagers, 1 bordar, 2 sokemen (0.5)
Cockerington		Ilbert (2)	7 villagers, 4 smallholders, 27 sokemen (3)
Alvingham			4 sokemen (1)
Aby		Wadard (1)	12 villagers, 4 sokemen, 2 smallholders (2.5)
Strubby			5 sokemen, 4 villagers (2)
Rigsby		Losoard (1)	5 villagers, 3 smallholders (0.5)
Well			1 sokeman, 2 villagers (?)
Ailby			3 sokemen, 2 smallholders (1)
Tothby			3 sokemen (1) = 3 oxen
Ashby Puerorum	1		9 villagers, 2 smallholders, 14 sokemen (3)
Bag Enderby & Markby			14 sokemen, 10 villagers, 1 bordar (2)
Ashby		Ilbert (0.5)	2 villagers, 2 smallholders, 8 sokemen (1)
Brigsley, Waithe, Ravendale			13 sokemen, 10 villagers (4)
Laceby, Bradley, Scartho	3		4 villagers, 5 smallholders, 85 sokemen (13.5)
Great Grimsby			55 sokemen, 1 villein (6)
Withcall		Ilbert (1)	4 villagers, 42 sokemen (6)
Stewton		Ilbert (1)	1 bordar
Owersby		Wadard (1)	5 villagers, 4 smallholders, 26 sokemen (5)
Thorganby	1		
Dry Doddington		Baldric	has 2 villagers, 2 smallholders (1)
Claypole	1		6 villagers, 2 smallholders *(1.5)*
Casthorpe		Sveinn	has 5 villagers, 1 bordar (1)
Stapleford		Thorr (1)	3 villagers, 1 bordar (1)
Canwick		Ilbert (2)	2 ?, 1 bordar
Owmby		Ilbert and Wadard (1 + 5 oxon)	

32 *Plough team.*

This table shows that a quarter of the Bishop's land in over 80 Lincolnshire villages was let to Ilbert, the 'bishop's man'. Others, who were sub-tenants, were listed as villagers, smallholders or sokemen. This table shows only arable land, which is indicated as 'plough land', a nominal measure of the amount of land which would require one plough team of eight oxen to plough per year. We can gain only a broad idea of the amount of arable land in a village, as an assessment of the total amount must allow for the fact that other principal tenants may have held land there. This example illustrates the point. At Ingham, the Bishop of Lincoln's man had five ploughing oxen, and one villager and one sokeman had six oxen. Also Roger of Poitou had three sokemen, two smallholders and one villager with one plough. Kolsveinn, who was Rainer of Bremeux's man, had land for half a plough. In addition, three villagers and two smallholders had five oxen. Lastly, Earnine held land directly from the king and had one villager and one sokeman with two oxen. The inter-relationship of land tenure in villages was very complex, and these different holdings formed large estates. Only when the arable land is assessed with mills, meadow, woodland and pasture can the viability of the manor as the basic unit of economic life be seen. Despite the changes in land tenure by 1086, it did not herald massive changes for the majority of the population. For most, life carried on much as before, but under new Norman lords.

6

Religious Houses in the Age of Faith

At the beginning of the third millennium it is difficult for us to understand how important religion was in medieval life. Alongside William I's military conquest came religious reform and with it a resurgence of religious fervour. The development of Lincoln Cathedral over some two and a half centuries was an embodiment of the development and strengthening of faith and, indeed, the ability of human beings to express their perception of heaven and earth, good and evil, in a building which, even now, remains one of the most impressive in the world. Most major changes at Lincoln Cathedral were brought about by catastrophe—first in 1141 when the original wooden roof burned down and was replaced by stone vaulting, whose weight—and a failure to strengthen the walls and perhaps a minor earthquake—caused major damage in 1185 when the nave collapsed. Once again the cathedral was rebuilt and was later extended through the city walls to inter the mortal remains of saintly Bishop Hugh, who died in 1200. Lincoln Cathedral survives today, but was only one of a number of magnificent buildings in Lincolnshire which were built to the glory of God. Each change at Lincoln represents not only the growing wealth of the church but a new and more intense phase in man's perception of God. For example, when the central tower collapsed in 1237 it was not only rebuilt, but built higher; in 1311 it was capped with a spire of oak and lead rising to a height of 160 metres, making it the highest building in the world. Standing on the top of a hill, dominating the city and the surrounding area for miles around, it must have truly appeared to be touching heaven.

33 *Lincoln Cathedral dominating the city as it has for more than 900 years.*

An indication of the relevance of religion to everyday life is that rich men were often willing to provide substantial sums of money to establish religious houses, where men and women could pass their lives performing religious services and in

contemplation according to the code of a particular denomination. Prior to the Conquest, monasteries had been founded at Bardney, Partney, Crowland, Barrow-on-Humber, and possibly at Kirton, but these all perished during the Viking invasions. Crowland was re-founded in the 10th century and certainly existed in 1066, but the status of the others is uncertain. By the Domesday Survey of 1086 there were probably three small cells containing 'alien' monks at Winghale in South Kelsey from St Sees, at Hougham from St Sever and Covenham from St Cerileph. Bardney was re-founded on a substantial scale in 1087. This was only the beginning and, by the end of the 12th century, 43 religious houses had been founded. Some 23 of them were founded during the troubled reign of Stephen (1135-54). Over the following two centuries a further 67 abbeys, friaries, priories as well as hospitals and colleges were established.

34 *A Cistercian monk.*

All the monastic orders, except the Cluniacs, were represented in Lincolnshire, encouraged perhaps by the relative solitude of 'unclaimed swamp' in such large areas of the county. The first were the Benedictines, who established a number of monasteries and one small nunnery at Stainfield. The monasteries at Bardney, Crowland and Spalding were of considerable size, while smaller houses were founded at Humberston, Sandtoft, Skendleby, Freiston, Deeping St James, Lincoln, and two at Stamford and Boston. Other orders were quick to establish their communities. Augustinians, who followed the teaching of St Augustine, founded their first house at Colchester around the beginning of the 12th century. Between about 1132, when the house at Wellow near Grimsby was founded, and the late 1180s, other communities had risen at Hyrst in Crowle, Thornton, Thornholm, Nocton Park, Torksey, Elsham, South Kyme, Markby, Newstead near Stamford, Bourne and Grimsby. The motivation for funding these first houses was religious, but by the middle of the 12th century, at a time of social upheaval, a level of cynicism had developed and the rich and powerful were beginning to endow monasteries as a way, as they saw it, of ensuring their entry to heaven. Some motives were even more down to earth: to enclose and improve land, implement drainage and, as in the case of the small priory at Holland Bridge, the inmates were expected to maintain the causeway from Kesteven to mid Holland. Even at this early stage there was some concern about the lifestyle that some of these rich institutions were enjoying. As a reaction against this, a more 'puritan' order of Cistercian houses developed. These at Kirkstead, Louth Park, Revesby, Swineshead and Vaudey near Edenham were to become some of the largest and most influential in the county. The Cistercians were initially hostile to women and thus had no nunneries. However, by the mid-13th century attitudes had changed and seven nunneries, which had been founded independently at Legbourne, Greenfield, Stixwould, Nuncoton, Gokewell, Fosse and Haynings, had become Cistercian houses. The Gilbertine order, the only order of English origin, was established by St Gilbert of Sempringham in 1131. Initially this was to have been a Cistercian order, but in 1147 Pope Eugenius entrusted the new order to its benefactor. Twenty-six Gilbertine houses

were founded nationally, of which 11 were in Lincolnshire at, for example, Haverholm, St Catherine's [Lincoln], Bullington, Alvingham, Sixhills, North Ormsby, Catley, Tunstall, and Newstead. The new order of Premonstratensian houses was first established in England at Newhouse in about 1143 and was soon followed by a further four abbeys—Barlings, Tupholme, Neubo, and Hagnaby—and a further one for nuns at Orford. One Carthusian house was established at Axholme at the end of the 14th century.

Most religious houses were founded in the lowlands of the county, particularly along the river Witham valley, east of Lincoln down onto the Fen edge, but also in the river Ancholme valley, the Isle of Axholme and the coastal marshes. These poorly drained and sparsely populated areas not only provided solitude for devotion but plenty of land. A cynic might say that a donation of such land on the part of a benefactor would not constitute very much of a gift. On the other hand, monasteries were probably alone in having the motivation, organisation and resources to bring such land into productive agricultural use. They became principal commercial organisations in the county, selling salt, cheese, leather and flour. Wool production was, however, the major activity of some 35 religious houses in the 13th century. Kirkstead, Revesby and Spalding were major exporters to Flanders and as far away as Italy. In 1313 Thornton Abbey's income was derived from 27 farms. The wealth of some of these monasteries could be seen in the magnificence of their buildings. Unfortunately, little remains for us to see—nothing on the scale of the ruins of Fountains and Rievaulx Abbeys in Yorkshire. Destruction during the Reformation means that our knowledge of the extent of the buildings is largely based on archaeological research. Louth Park Abbey, for example, was at its prime the largest Cistercian house in the country and contained a church which was 78 metres long. Barlings Abbey church was over 91 metres long and rose above the flat countryside as a powerful symbol of faith and control for miles around. In addition, so called 'Alien' houses were established by all the Orders except the Carthusians. Some religious houses were established for other reasons. Most notable among these, and of great importance in Lincolnshire, were the military orders of Knights Hospitaller and Knights Templar who built to aid pilgrims travelling to and from the Holy Land. These orders caught the public mood and became extremely rich through donations and bequests, with foundations at Willoughton, Eagle, Aslackby and Temple Bruer. There were Hospitaller houses at Maltby and Skirbeck and Lincoln.

35 *North Kyme Cross.*

By the beginning of the 13th century it can be argued that monasteries had begun to lose their religious ideal. They were increasingly seen as being spiritually and physically divorced from those they were supposed to serve and had become commercial organisations and retreats for the wealthy. During the 13th century a new religious fervour was introduced to England by friars following the teaching of St Francis of Assisi in Italy and Spain's St Dominic, who independently sought a less comfortable

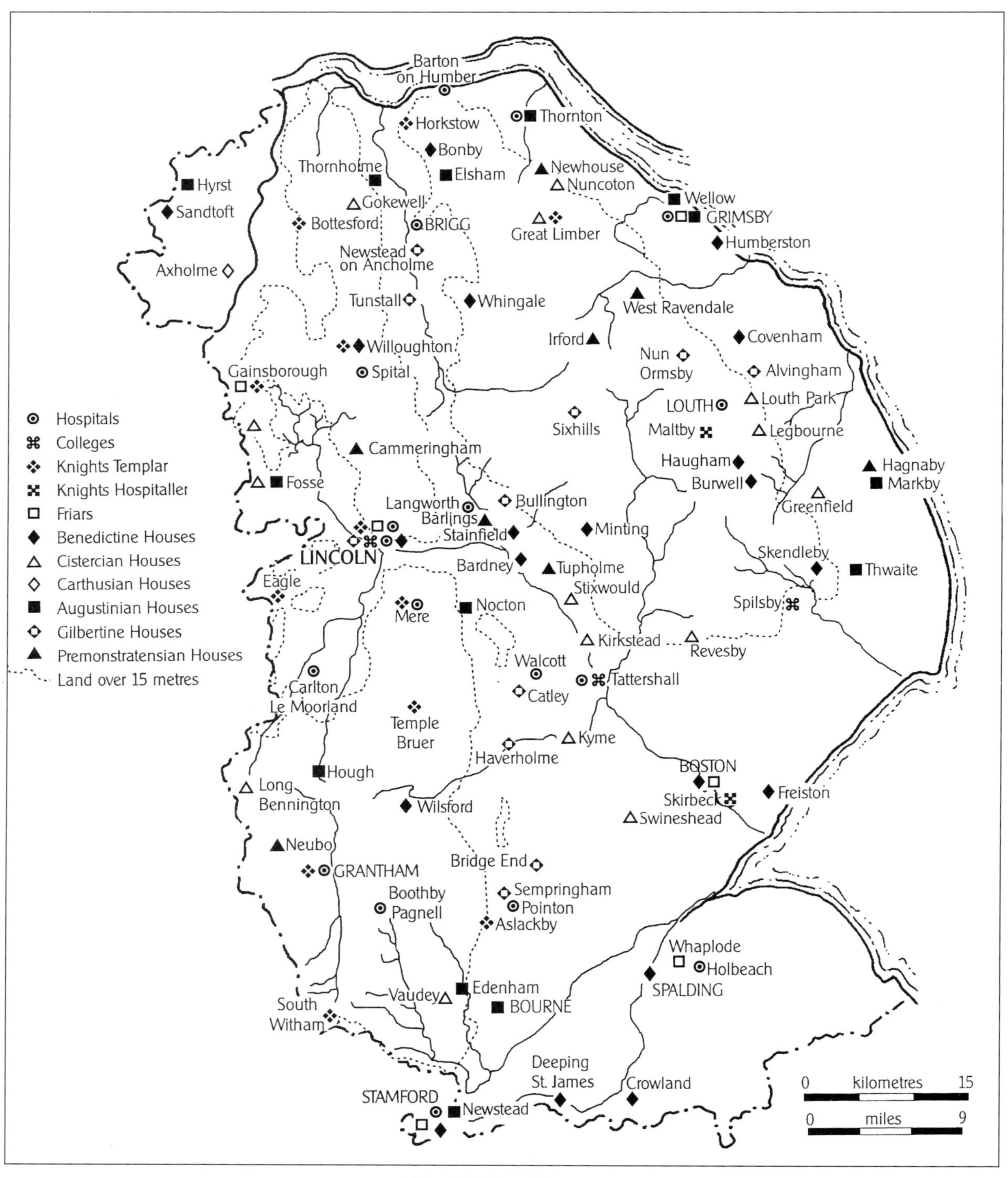

36 *Religious Houses.*

and more active way of living a Christian life. These mendicant friars, representing a number of orders, were to be found in the larger towns. In addition to Dominican and Franciscan friars, Augustinian, Carmelite and Friars of the Sack were located at Lincoln and Stamford; Dominican (Black), Franciscan (Grey), Augustinian and Carmelite (White) at Boston, and Franciscan and Augustinian at Grimsby and a short-lived single house of Crutched Friars at Whaplode. Although these were usually small houses, this did not nullify their vigour in preaching throughout the county in churches and in the open air. Perhaps, because of their town location and austere lifestyle little physical evidence of these friars remains today, although the nave of the early Franciscan church survives, next to the Central Library in Lincoln. Despite the high ideals which heralded the beginning of this movement, it too became more concerned with the mortal life than the life hereafter. However, much good was done. Lincoln, as other towns, had religious foundations which provided for the needs of the community—hospitals, schools, charity for the sick and old as well as shelter for pilgrims, particularly after the death of Bishop Hugh, who came in large numbers to pray at his tomb in the newly enlarged cathedral. These religious houses were some of the most substantial buildings in the county.

By 1086 there had already been a boom in church building throughout the county, and some 255 had been founded (out of an eventual total of around 700). These are some of the glories of the county that can be seen today and grew from two main sources. First, those which developed from Minster churches were often at the centre of royal estates such as Horncastle, Grantham and possibly Caistor. In the surrounding area, or *parochia*, there may have been a number of subsidiary chapels. The major development, however, corresponds with the Norman settlement, when the pre-Conquest royal, ecclesiastic and aristocratic settlements were broken up at the same time as villages began to evolve as distinct social units. Churches were often built by large landowners to serve their families and tenants. For example, Baldwin fitz Gilbert rebuilt the church at Bourne, Henry fitz Eudo at Kirkstead, Ivo Tailbois at Spalding, Alan de Creoun at Frieston and Bishop Alexander of Lincoln at Sleaford, along with his castle there. As with monasteries, endowments and gifts to churches often had strings attached. Henry of Longchamp endowed the altar at Burton Pedwardine and gave the vicar three acres of land on the condition that mass was said for him and his heirs every week. The development of new churches in villages

Boston, (alias Botolphs Town,) Situate near the Mouth of the River Witham, in Latitude 53:2 and Longitude 0:5 East
of the Meridian of London. Is a Considerable large
Town having in it Several fair Buildings. It has
two Markets Weekly. Viz. on Wednesday and Saturday
and two Fairs Yearly. Viz. on the 23d. of April and 25th.
of July, and a Mart which is Proclaim'd on the 30th of Novemb:
for nine days. It is well Supply'd with Fish from the
Sea and the River, and Fowl from the Neighbouring Fens.
and Carries on a Considerable Trade in Merchandize.
The Church is a very Beautiful Fabrick, Especially
the Tower which is Justly Admir'd for its Curious Work-
manship and Height. It is a good Seamark being
Seen at a great distance at Sea. The Altitude of
the Steeple and Length of the Church are Equal Viz.
94 Yards. It has Steps 365. Windows 52. and Pillars 12
It is a Town Corporate. Govern'd by a Mayor, Recorder, 12 Aldermn.
and 18 Common Council men. It Sends two Members to Parliament
Who are at this time Lord Ver. Bertie & John Michel Esq.
THE SOUTH VIEW of the CHURCH.

37 *The church of St Botolph, Boston, from an illustration of 1741.*

38 *The Jews House, Lincoln built about 1160.*

eventually led to the formation of parishes, which by the early 12th century had become well established, although during the Norman period the manor rather than the parish was still the smallest unit of administration.

Religious houses were affected by booms and slumps in the economy. In the 1320s there was a general decline in trade which amongst other things caused a fall in the price of wool resulting in considerable hardship. They were able to borrow some money from the Jewish community which was to be found in Lincoln and Stamford until in 1290 it was expelled by Edward I. Kirkstead, Louth Park and Revesby abbeys had been indebted to money lender Aaron of Lincoln. Add to this the effects of the Black Death in 1349. Religious houses were particularly badly hit because of the communal life of monasteries and of their work in caring for the sick and dying. As a result they were so weakened that many never regained their former position. By the second half of the 14th century, some religious houses were so small that they could only just survive. A survey of 42 religious houses in 1376 shows that 13 had fewer than 10 'religious', and at Eagle and Hough there were only two brothers. By the time Henry VIII set about the dissolution of the religious houses in the 1530s many had declined to a shadow of their former role and position. The fact that Henry VIII and Thomas Cromwell were able to oppose them in such a direct manner is a clear indication that they were no longer the vital force of earlier centuries.

7

Medieval Trade and Commerce

During the two and a half centuries after the Norman Conquest, Lincolnshire enjoyed a substantial economic boom, as a result of its position on the eastern side of England with a coast facing mainland Europe, diverse geology, important monasteries and relatively large urban and other populated centres. With the exception of Lincoln whose population in 1086 was more than 5,000 and Stamford with 2-3,000 population, the boom towns lay on the coast and in the Fens. Estimates suggest that Sutton in Holland's population by 1332 had increased to over 5,000, Pinchbeck to between 4 and 4,500, and Spalding, Moulton, Weston and Fleet to about 3,000. The availability of land and the opportunity to engage in livestock husbandry, salt making, fishing and fowling brought about this situation. These were some of the largest concentrations of population in England, but because they remained agriculturally based they are not classified as towns, unlike Stamford, which had the characteristics of an urban centre, where almost 60 per cent of households were involved in commerce as shopkeepers, merchants or dealers and a significant number of leather-workers. The rest were victuallers, publicans or skilled artisans. Only 6 per cent were agricultural workers. Lincoln supported a number of trades associated with cloth production, leather-working, construction, shipping, clothing, haberdashery and victualling. Most Lincolnshire people, however, inhabited villages and hamlets whose sustainability depended largely on the quality of the soil. Generally, compared with Holland, Kesteven was less wealthy, whilst the uplands of Lindsey were relatively poor, a fact reflected in the Domesday Survey.

The economy of medieval Lincolnshire was agriculturally based and most people made their livelihood from the land or in some craft or industry related directly to farming. For most people the farming year dictated a natural rhythm of rural life. Those who worked directly on the land had seasonal jobs—ploughing, sowing, harvesting, threshing. The state of the harvest dictated the quality of their winter existence. Animal husbandry also had its own rhythm. Extensive flocks of sheep pastured on the marshland and fens for most of the year. Lambing occurred in the spring and shearing in the summer. Cattle were to be found on the clays and marshlands and

39 *Nun Coton plough.*

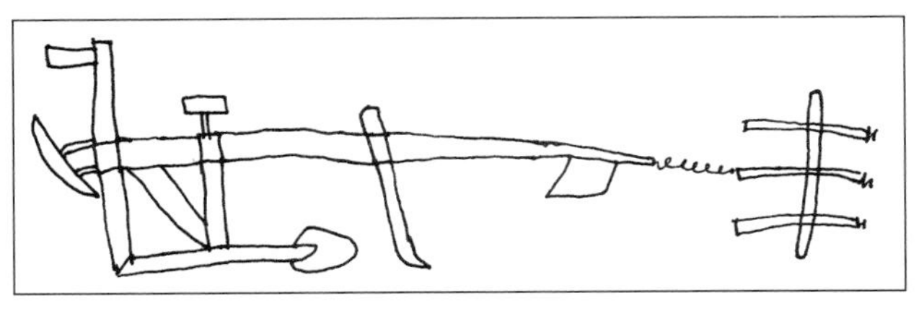

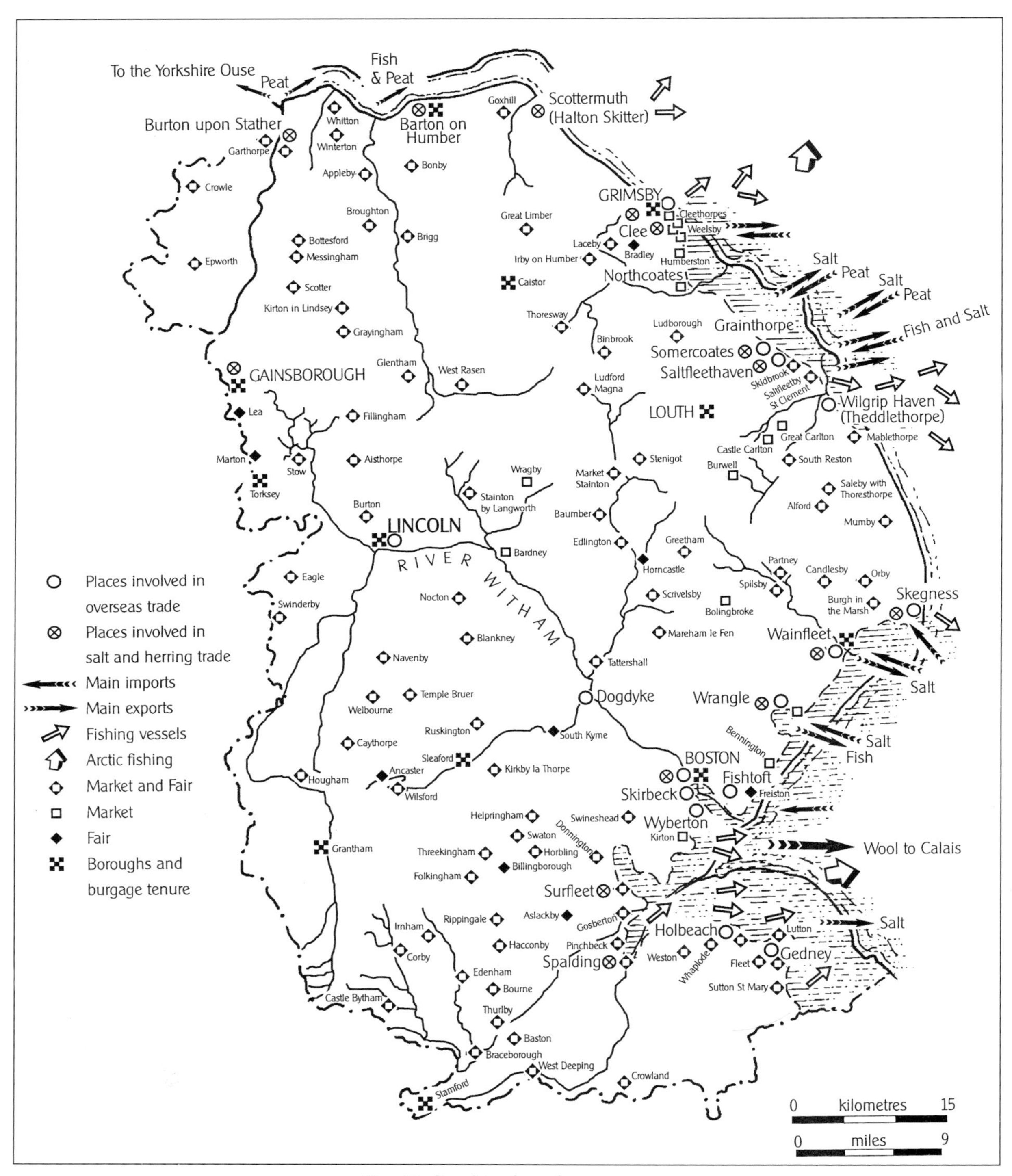

40 *Medieval trade and commerce.*

41 *Windmill.*

were killed and salted in the autumn for the winter. Even those jobs common to most villages, such as brewing and thatching, had their own seasonal activities based on the availability of natural resources.

Medieval villages looked very different from the villages of today. Most consisted of a number of dwellings around the church. It was unusual to find farm houses located in fields away from the centre of the village. Around the village were two or three large open fields where individuals farmed on land divided into furlong or 'furrow-long' lengths. One noticeable aspect of these open fields was the absence of hedges separating individual holdings, which gave the impression of a wide open space. One example of such a field system was at Castle Bytham. Based on an assessment of the property of Margaret, widow of Edmund de Colevill, received on her husband's death in 1316, it is possible to estimate that the total land in the village was about 780 acres with the North Field comprising 227 acres, the South Field 338 acres and the West Field 199 acres. Fields were rotated yearly with two fields being cropped and the third field left fallow with roaming livestock fertilising the ground for cultivation the following year. Most villages had mixed farming containing arable, meadow, pasture and woodland. Woods were particularly important, since they provided firewood, timber for building and domestic items as well as somewhere for pigs to forage. However, woodland in Lincolnshire was relatively scarce; only about 5 per cent of the county was given over to forests which were mainly on the eastern slopes of the Wolds, the central clay lands of south Lindsey, south Kesteven and the river Trent valley. Many villages had their own bakers and brewers, who produced the staple diet, and there were often thatchers and carpenters. Blacksmiths were also common and carried out a valued trade. They appear to have been better off financially than most, making farm tools with iron from north Lindsey, and imported to the county from Derbyshire and Northamptonshire. Villages should not always be seen as being separate and independent as parishes were later to become. Indeed, as described in Chapter 5, they were often just part of a manor, which was a larger economic unit.

Regional agricultural differences existed. The three parts of the county—Lindsey, Kesteven and Holland—having different topographical and geological characteristics led to some agricultural specialisation. Soil quality dictated which crops were grown—usually wheat, barley or oats, and the type of animal husbandry carried on. One account of these regional variations comes from the evidence of Edward I's Parliament of February 1301, which was held at Lincoln. He ordered Hugh de Bussey, the sheriff of Lincolnshire, to obtain enough provisions for one month. This amounted to 800 quarters of wheat, 400 of malt, 1,000 of oats, 200 cows and oxen, 700 sheep, 160 pigs and hay for 400 horses. Kesteven appears to have been a major producer of wheat. Cattle came from the marshlands and the Fen edge. Swine were particularly numerous in the woodlands of Kesteven and south Lindsey and sheep from the large flock on the Wolds and uplands north and south of Lincoln. West Lindsey produced large quantities of oats and some mutton was produced in the

42 *Sheepfold.*

Isle of Axholme. Where land-owners had dispersed estates there could be further specialisation. Henry de Lacy, of Bolingbroke, owned substantial estates throughout Lincolnshire from Brocklesby in the north to Sutton in the south, as well as property in Cheshire, Lancashire and Yorkshire. His Lincolnshire estates were on the whole geared to the production of grain crops; stock rearing was undertaken in Lancashire and wool production in Yorkshire. Wheat and barley were the principal crops mainly on the thinner, well drained lands of the chalk Wolds and limestone Lincoln cliff but also on the higher land at the fen edge in the parishes of Swaton and Horbling. In contrast oats, which were suitable to the wetter arable conditions of the Fens, were grown in large quantities at Donington. All parishes had pigs and, although Lacy's Yorkshire estates had extensive herds of sheep, they were also to be found in most of his Lincolnshire parishes with the exception of those in the Fens.

The 13th-century boom in agricultural activity happened largely because of a substantial increase in the population, which in turn stimulated agricultural production leading to a period of 'high farming'. Thus a number of parishes were extended to bring into cultivation marginal land, particularly in the Wash and coastal Lindsey areas and also on the edges of the Fens. There was also increased investment in new technology. The Domesday Survey refers to 380 water-mills, but they were not suitable for use in much of the south of the county because of a lack of fast-flowing rivers and streams. Windmills were used from the 12th century. They could be located almost anywhere and had a revolutionary effect on the developing local economy. The increased wealth from agriculture encouraged many local magnates to invest in their salvation by endowing their local churches, which resulted in a golden age of church building. St Mary Magdalen at Gedney, St Peter and Paul at Algarkirk and, of course, St Botolph's at Boston are fine examples. Wealth from the wool trade paid for much of this church building and the production of wool was the most important industry throughout the Middle Ages. At the end of the 13th century it was in demand by Flemish, Italian and German merchants, and developed from a small-scale cottage industry to a large-scale urban operation organised by agents and entrepreneurs. Monasteries were major producers. Sheep can be grazed in the fenland, marshlands and on the desolate tops of the Wolds, so it suited the location of many monasteries. Thornton Abbey on the northern edge of the Wolds, for example, had 7,453 sheep in 1313. Sheep provided a better option than large-scale arable farming not only because the land was better suited for pasture, but sheep do not require constant tending.

43 *Medieval ship.*

Along the length of Lincolnshire's coast were ports and havens from which to pursue coastal and European trade which were of growing importance throughout the Middle Ages. The river Witham was navigable from Lincoln to Boston thus providing a link, via the Fosse Dyke canal which was made navigable again in 1121, with the river Trent and thereby enhancing the status of Torksey as a port. This route became a major highway; by the Middle Ages river transport was particularly important

44 *The church of St Botolph shows every indication of Boston's medieval prosperity.*

for the trade in wool from the midland counties. In Lincolnshire salt production remained important throughout this period. The process has had a lasting impact on the landscape between Tetney and North Somercotes, where it has left a patchwork of irregular mounds over 18 square kilometres. Production was large-scale. After the spring tide the top layer of salt-impregnated sand was collected and washed in a clay-lined pit with peat at the bottom, which separated the brine from the sand. The brine was boiled leaving the salt. The waste was piled up and, as the mounds became too large, the salt makers moved closer to the sea resulting in substantial land reclamation.

At the beginning of the 12th century Boston was the premier port in the kingdom, surpassing London and Southampton. Up to 43 per cent of the total amount of wool exported from England was sent via Boston. Some wool was brought by coasters from East Anglia and Yorkshire, but much was transported along the river network from the midland producers of Derbyshire and Nottinghamshire. Lincolnshire monastic houses were also major producers. In addition to wool, large quantities of locally finished cloth and lead from Derbyshire were exported. Grimsby was also a significant port shipping goods to Scandinavia but not at this time involved with deep-sea fishing. Wainfleet was developing as an important port, servicing a river trade from the southern Wolds along the river Steeping, and there were ports at Skegness and at Saltfleethaven used extensively by Louth Park Abbey. Scandinavian, Flemish and Hanseatic vessels used these ports and havens to import timber, cloth, stockfish and wine, in return for grain, cloth and wool. The port of Spalding relied on the navigability of the river Welland. The river Ancholme was navigable from its mouth into the river Humber to Bishopbridge near Market Rasen, although it is not known whether these rivers were navigable throughout the year.

Apart from the high level of commercial activity involved in international trade, for most people economic activity took place within the county at markets and fairs. From the 11th century, England became a cash-using society and markets and fairs provided an opportunity to sell increasing agricultural surpluses and to exchange goods for money—to pay rents and for other necessities. By the middle of the 14th century there were 120 official charter markets, and there were probably many others. No village was likely to be further than five miles from a market and many villagers had a choice. Official market status was obtained by charters granted by the king in return for a fee, and controlled by the local lords of the manor who were keen to enhance the local economy. They could also regulate the

market and exact a toll from traders. Some traders would have been itinerant, regularly attending different markets in an area, as still happens today. Others were local crafts people and villagers, who could sell the produce from their holding. The locations of 88 markets are known, distributed throughout the county with the greatest density in the Fens, Fen edge villages and south Kesteven, which is indicative of the relative wealth of this area. Ten Fen townships had two markets a week and at Lincoln a market was held on Monday, Wednesday and Friday. Other villages held markets once a week, on any day except Sunday. Weekly markets provided an opportunity for local trade. Fairs were on a much larger scale and became a focal point for merchants from greater distances and included imported commodities. At Boston, for example, there were luxuries like furs, silks, wines, hawks and spices and bulk items such as timber, sea coal, and pitch as well as a greater variety of general merchandise not always available at weekly markets. As with markets, fairs were established by charter and were located throughout the county. Some places had two fairs a year lasting a number of days. Most were held between May and June, thus avoiding bad weather and harvest time. Fairs, too, were more numerous in the Holland and Kesteven areas, with fewer on the Wolds of Lindsey. Most of the major fairs linked with water transport either on the coast—as at Skidbrooke, Grimsby, Wainfleet and Barton—or on rivers—as at Boston, Lincoln, Spalding, Pinchbeck, Spilsby, Horncastle, Tattershall and Torksey. All these had two fairs a year. In the booming 12th and 13th centuries fairs and markets were an integral part of Lincolnshire's vibrant economy. However by the 16th century the number of markets and fairs had declined, becoming concentrated in market towns such as Sleaford, Bourne, Horncastle, Spilsby, Louth and Boston. Lincolnshire became a county of market towns, most of which survive today. Fairs as trading centres declined, too, although some specialised

45 *The deserted village of Calcethorpe showing houses, garden plots and typical ridge and furrow of the open field system.*

46 *Horse and cart.*

fairs, such as the Boston sheep fair and the Horncastle horse fair, lasted well into the 19th century.

At the end of the 13th century the economy of the county started to decline from being one of the most prosperous regions in the country. This was due to a mixture of natural and man-made factors which produced a slump that did not begin to be reversed until the 18th century. A series of poor wet summers resulted in bad harvests, so bad that substantial flooding in the Fens caused much of the marginal land, brought into cultivation during the boom periods of the previous 100 years, to become unproductive. Flooding extended along the Lindsey coastal marshes, the river Ancholme valley and along the vale of Trent, all causing widespread famine. Climate changes also brought coastal and river silting. Changes in farming practice, whereby land had been enclosed for sheep pasture to the detriment of arable farming, also reduced the economic viability of village communities. By the end of the 13th century transport along the Fosse Dyke canal and the river Witham was again difficult and access to Boston from the sea was impeded. Twice in the 14th century Commissions were held to inquire into the condition of the Fosse Dyke. The situation was not improved by making Lincoln in 1326 one of eight staple ports through which all exports of wool, hide, skins and tin had to pass. This provided a short-lived boost to the local economy but 15 years later the traffic was transferred to Boston. This meant that 200 or so wool weavers, active in Lincoln at the end of the 13th century, had disappeared by the 1330s. The level of raw wool exports through Boston declined throughout the 14th century. The whole situation was made worse by the wars waged during the reign of Edward II against the Scots, Welsh and the French. Whilst wars place burdens on any population, the war with France in particular was a disaster for trade.

When in 1349 the Black Death arrived in Lincolnshire, the economic down-turn was already well advanced. Its impact was enormous. Up to 45 per cent of the population died, reducing the county's population from about 385,000 to about 212,000 in 1350. The death rate was uneven throughout the county. The Louth Park chronicle reports that, 'This scourge in many places left less than a fifth part of the population surviving ...'. The viability of many villages with a reduced population became difficult and in some cases they were soon abandoned. Some, such as West Wykeham, North Cadeby, Brackenborough, Maidenwell, Walmsgate, Biscathorpe and Brauncewell, can still be identified by aerial photography today as bumps in the ground. The economy and the population did begin to recover after the Black Death, but its impact, combined with changing trading and economic patterns, contributed to the county's economic decline over the following four centuries.

8
The Reformation

At the beginning of the 16th century the relationship between the Catholic church and the people of Lincolnshire was extremely close. There were over 700 parishes each with a church or chapel and priest. The church was at the centre of the parish both physically and psychologically. Church spires or towers could be seen from almost anywhere in the parish, and the church was part of the daily lives of parishioners. Feast days, saints days and holidays formed part of the church's calendar, providing a rare opportunity for leisure away from the daily toil. Many tradesmen earned their living from work associated with improvements to and the upkeep of probably the largest building in the parish. They were involved in administering alms for the poor and providing schools and hospitals. Many parish churches were wealthy as it had become common practice for money and other riches to be bequeathed to them. Some of this money found its way into improving the fabric of the building. For example, at Louth between 1501 and 1515, £305 was spent on a new spire to make it the tallest parish church spire in the county. This major project required not only the expertise of local tradesmen, thereby boosting the local economy, but also expenditure outside the parish, since the stone was quarried at Wilsford near Ancaster, transported by water, via the river Slea and the river Bain, to Coningsby, and then carted to Louth. In addition to the parish churches, there were some 80 other religious houses spread throughout the county. This medieval religious revival (see Chapter 6) meant that by the beginning of the 16th century, though some had declined, many other religious houses were still extremely rich and powerful. Henry VIII's long battle with Pope Clement VII and the Catholic church over his divorce (from Catherine of Aragon to marry Ann Boleyn) was to have severe repercussions on the whole country and not least on Lincolnshire, because many in the county took particular exception to the king's actions.

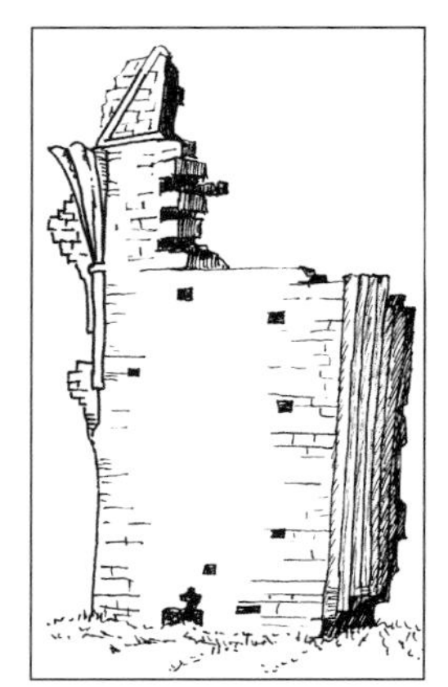

47 *All that remains of Barlings Abbey.*

The rising in Lincolnshire was caused by a groundswell of public opinion fearful of the uncertainty caused by change. By 1536 the first 20 smaller religious houses, those valued at less than £200, had already been suppressed. This was witnessed by local people and was seen not only as an assault on the buildings themselves but also on their own belief. Roofs were removed so that the lead could be sold, the stairs and battlements were demolished and anything of value from the interior was

48 *Louth Park Abbey, 1726.*

taken for sale. They were not entirely demolished because of the expense, but any stones were to be sold in the future as required. This was only the beginning. Another subsidy had been allowed by parliament to establish an enquiry into the quality of the clergy. This again affected public attitudes. Nowhere was this more evident than at Louth, where the Rev. Thomas Kendall mentioned at the church service on 1 October 1536 that the commissioners appointed by Thomas, Lord Cromwell, Henry's chief minister, were at Caistor to begin their assessment of the quality of the local clergy. These included members of the local gentry: Thomas Moigne from North Willingham, Sir Edward Maddison from Fonaby and Lord Burgh from Gainsborough. The people of Louth were the first to rise. It seems the catalyst was to protect the property of *their* church, particularly the gold and silver which they considered was community property. This action was quickly followed by a large number of the general population at Horncastle, Spilsby and Alford.

These events occurred simultaneously in a number of towns, suggesting that there must have been widespread disquiet at the actions of the commissioners, who were taken by a mob to Louth where in fear of their lives they were forced to swear an oath to 'Almighty God, to Christ's Catholic Church, to our Sovereign Lord the King, and unto the Commons of this realm, so help you God and Holydon and by this book.' The atmosphere was tense at Louth, Caistor and also at Alford, but there was little actual violence apart from an official being put in the stocks. However, at Horncastle things took a more serious turn. Two officials, including the King's commissioner Dr. Rayne, were killed by the mob apparently led by the priest. These first few chaotic days of mob violence in the market towns of the central and southern Wolds soon gave way to a more ordered series of events. What began as an unplanned and incoherent popular uprising, spurred on by some parish and church authorities and individual trades people, by the fourth day became more

organised through the help of leading members of the Lincolnshire gentry, most notably Sir William Maddison, Sir Robert Tyrwhit, Sir Robert Dymoke and Robert and Sir John Sutton. They were later to deny their compliance to avoid accusations of treason, pleading that they were forced to take part. Their motives were indeed questionable; undoubtedly a number were threatened, but many took the opportunity presented to them by a popular uprising to take their collective grievances to the king. By the sixth day, in the region of 12,000 insurgents had mustered at Grange de Lings in the parish of Riseholme, a few miles north of Lincoln.

Four days into the rebellion the king had been informed and was beginning to act. Unable to rely on the Lincolnshire gentry, Henry obtained a force under the command of the Duke of Suffolk who headed for the county, reaching Stamford on 12 October. Lord John Hussey of Sleaford, the most eminent man in the county, was in his 70s and, on hearing that up to 500 people were on their way to return with him to Lincoln, forcibly if necessary, he fled to Nottingham. Unfortunately for Hussey, his inaction was seen by the king as an act of betrayal. He was also known to be against the religious changes and a supporter of Catherine of Aragon. This was his undoing. He was beheaded in Lincoln for treason in summer 1537.

The king had the upper hand, despite support for the rebellion from other parts of the country, notably from Yorkshire. By the time the protesters reached Lincoln, some were already deserting back to their own villages. However, most were keen to pursue their demands and march on. They were only persuaded not to by the gentry, who were by now more aware of the dangerous ground on which they were treading until they heard the king's reply. There were arguments amongst the gentry in Lincoln about the framing of the demands. Despite the obsequious language of the final petition, Henry dismissed them out of hand, referring to the county as 'one of the most brute and beastly in the

49 *The church of the Knights Templar, Temple Bruer.*

realm'. Only 13 days after it had begun, the rebellion was over. Most of the common people received a general pardon but the ringleaders were hanged during the following few months at Horncastle, Louth and Lincoln.

These events in Lincolnshire did not delay the end of the monasteries. The rebellion and other similar events elsewhere in the country, notably the Yorkshire 'Pilgrimage of Grace', probably hastened their dissolution. The large religious houses of Barlings and Kirkstead were seen as supporters of the uprising and were thus immediately dissolved. Bardney followed soon after. The dissolution took its course and the original worries of the people of Louth came to fruition. St James, as all other churches, lost the gold and treasures to which the community attached such importance. Some monasteries surrendered themselves to the commissioners, many of whom were Lincolnshire gentry, such as Edward Dymoke and John Heneage, who had remained on the winning side during the rebellion. During the last few weeks of September and the beginning of October 1538 Sempringham, Haverholme, Catley, Bullington, Sixhills, Alvingham, Nunormsby and Newstead were closed, resulting in nearly £24,000 for the exchequer of which £8,000 were annual rents. By the end of 1539 all Lincolnshire's religious houses had gone.

Since Henry VIII himself could not manage all the dispersed ex-monastic lands throughout the country there was a redistribution of lands to those members of the gentry who had supported the king. This was to have far-reaching effects, since these new owners, such as the Custs of Pinchbeck, Skipworths of Ormsby, the Heneage family of Hainton and the Carr family of Sleaford, were to become leaders of county society in subsequent centuries. Acquisition of new land increased their social standing. The largest transfer of land, however, was to Charles Brandon, Duke of Suffolk. Not only had he played an important part in bringing the rebellion to an end, but he had the added advantage of being related to the king through marriage. He acquired properties from 16 religious houses, making him by far the leading land owner in Lincolnshire. Thomas Manners, the 1st Earl of Rutland, also acquired Lincolnshire monastic lands at the site of Belvoir Priory, just across the Leicestershire border. Numerous others seized their opportunity to obtain available lands—for example, Sir John Heneage, who already had connections with the abbey at Bardney as steward, the Tyrwhit family with Thornton and the Disney family with Belvoir Abbey lands held at Aubourn. The effect of the dissolution of the monasteries on the average person is less easy to determine. For many it meant no more than a change of landlord, as life carried on much as it had done before. For others, livings were made from the sale of stone, timber and lead as buildings were dismantled.

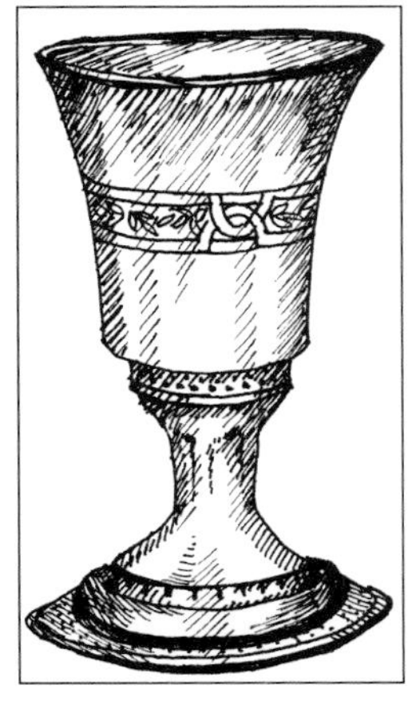

50 *Post-Reformation plate.*

Most people, however, would have been aware of the changes directly affecting their parish churches, whose character was changed by the substantial shift towards Protestantism during Edward VI's short reign (1547-53). They became altogether simpler places in line with the new religious order. Articles of church furniture, vessels and vestments, all of which were considered superstitious, were removed. Rood screens were

pulled down, the iconic statues and paintings were destroyed, and in some cases Mass books were burnt. There was the universal introduction of the English Bible. The Lincoln diocese was reduced, and large areas were transferred to the new Bishops of Oxford and Peterborough. The return to Catholic ways during the even shorter and bitter reign of Mary I (1553-8) was met in Lincolnshire without much comment, perhaps because there were still only a few Protestants in the county. Her policy did not have the same devastating impact as it did elsewhere in the realm. No Lincolnshire people were put to death although a small number, including John Aylmer, the archdeacon of Stow, and Nicholas Bullingham, the archdeacon of Lincoln, fled to Europe in fear of their lives. Seventy priests were removed from their parishes because they had married during Edward's reign.

Many reforms begun under Edward VI were reinstated under Elizabeth I. This time, despite the defence of their faith put up by the people of north Lincolnshire less than a generation earlier, there seems to have been little opposition in the county to the reinstatement of Protestant ways after 1559, perhaps because of the excesses of Mary I. Thomas Watson, as bishop of Lincoln the foremost churchman in the county, refused to submit to the new oath and accept the end of papal authority, but very few others followed. The year 1559 saw the final sweeping away of superstitious objects from churches. The survey, the *Inventarium Monumentorum Superstitionis*, listed all the adornments associated with the Catholic religion as practised in a parish church and they were finally removed. The papistical books at Bilsby were destroyed and the Mass books were sold, but some of the most sacred adornments were recycled. At Claxby Pluckacre and Cumberworth, vestments were made into dresses for players and at Walesby the holy water vat became a horse trough. Another major change was the introduction of a pulpit and pews, because preaching was a feature of the reformed services. Churches began to assume the characteristics of the Anglican church of today.

The Elizabethan settlement—the policy of a middle course between religious extremes pursued in 1559-62—seems to have been broadly accepted in the county. In 1664 Bishop Bullingham was asked to provide the government with a confidential report on the leading Lincolnshire inhabitants. Of 69 listed people only 14 were described as 'hinderers', compared with 24 described as 'indifferent' and 31 as 'earnest in religion'. The middle way sought by Elizabeth failed as extremists—Puritans and Jesuits—came to the fore, which made compromise impossible. For the next century, Puritan ideology was in the ascendancy and almost destroyed any remaining Catholic adherence.

9

The Civil War

The part played by Lincolnshire during the English Civil War owes more to its geographical position—between main regions of Parliamentary support and the Royalist strongholds at Newark just across the Nottinghamshire border, and to a lesser extent at Belvoir in Leicestershire—than to the stance taken by its people. On balance, however, Parliament had greater support at the commencement of the war as most of the 12 Members of Parliament sided with it, although with no real enthusiasm. Three issues religion, tax and drainage, can be seen as being particularly relevant. Religion again assumed a level of importance due to a perceived, if not actual, drift towards Catholicism at a time when Puritanism was an important force. Charles I had married the French Catholic princess, Henrietta Maria, and his appointment of William Laud as Archbishop of Canterbury in 1633 was to have the most disquieting effect in the countryside. Laud's attacks on Puritan priests and his insistence on returning to more superstitious religious practices caused anger. Boston was seen as a Puritan town. John Cotton, the vicar there from 1612, went to Boston, Massachusetts in 1633, after he became increasingly at odds with the return to old religious doctrines, and he joined there perhaps 250 of his own congregation. During the repression of the Puritans by James I, John Smith, a non-conformist minister from Gainsborough, joined others from Nottinghamshire and Yorkshire to sail from Boston to Holland in 1609. In 1620 they were to sail to found a new colony in America.

51 *Charles I.*

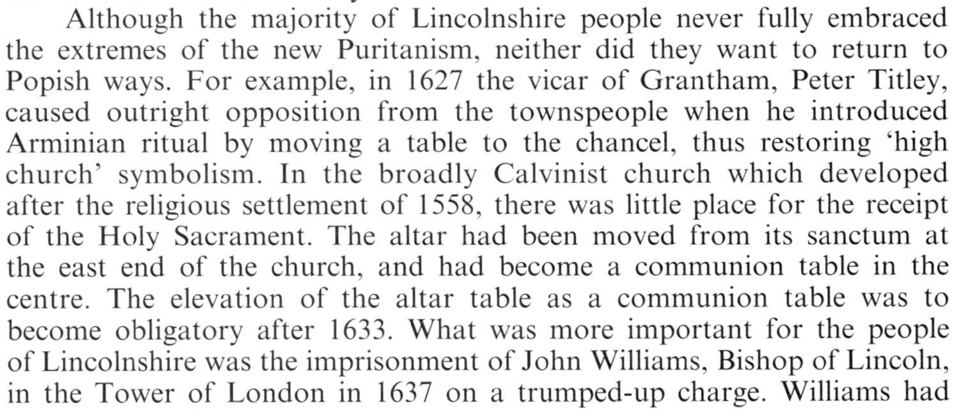

Although the majority of Lincolnshire people never fully embraced the extremes of the new Puritanism, neither did they want to return to Popish ways. For example, in 1627 the vicar of Grantham, Peter Titley, caused outright opposition from the townspeople when he introduced Arminian ritual by moving a table to the chancel, thus restoring 'high church' symbolism. In the broadly Calvinist church which developed after the religious settlement of 1558, there was little place for the receipt of the Holy Sacrament. The altar had been moved from its sanctum at the east end of the church, and had become a communion table in the centre. The elevation of the altar table as a communion table was to become obligatory after 1633. What was more important for the people of Lincolnshire was the imprisonment of John Williams, Bishop of Lincoln, in the Tower of London in 1637 on a trumped-up charge. Williams had

IV The Brayford Pool and Lincoln Cathedral *by John Wilson Carmichael, 1858.*

V *The nave at Lincoln Cathedral completed by Bishop Hugh.*

been a thorn in Laud's side for a number of years and his attack on Titley did not help him.

Whilst the king's personal influence through Archbishop Laud could be seen in spiritual matters, it was in secular affairs that his reign was most conspicuous and contested. The collection of ship money, a tax levied to fund the war against the Scots, was as unpopular in Lincolnshire as it was in other parts. Despite questions about the legality of the tax, during the first two years, 1635 and 1636, the full amount of £8,000 was collected. Over the next three years the tax became more unpopular and remained 82 per cent in arrears. Even the 1638 assessment of only £2,900 had a shortfall of 27 per cent. These are figures for the county, but the resistance was seen at the parish level, as it fell on the sheriff and local constables to collect the tax.

52 *A Parliamentary trooper.*

Drainage of parishes in the Fens and the Isle of Axholme often caused disputes over ownership of land and thus the amount of land eligible for assessment. It was here, where Charles had taken a direct hand in improvements, that he was most unpopular, so that, when the Civil War began, the area around Boston sided most strongly with Parliament. Oliver Cromwell, too, had opposed the enclosure and drainage of the Cambridgeshire Fens. Ancient agreements and traditional farming practices amongst Fen and Isle of Axholme farmers meant that, even though it was a progressive measure, it would meet with opposition. Much of the undrained area was rich common land which had supported for centuries a thriving local economy of fowling and fishing. Drainage schemes would destroy this. As a result, riots occurred at Pinchbeck, Donington, and one riot near Boston lasted three days where it was reported that large numbers of rioters had '... committed greate wast and destruction theire of wheate and other graine and behaved themselves furiously and outragiously'. At Bolingbroke, houses belonging to the undertakers and their servants were destroyed, dikes were filled in and crops worth £1,000 were devastated. Opposition in the Isle of Axholme was eventually bought off by a series of bribes which enabled the drainage contractors to proceed. However, the opposition in the Fens was the greatest and the king's close association with drainage did little for his public support. But, even here, simple generalisations cannot be made. Crowland persisted throughout both Civil Wars to support the King.

Both sides had their supporters and supporters needed a figurehead around whom to rally. Thus in 1642 Parliament appointed two lords lieutenant: the Earl of Lincoln and Lord Willoughby of Parham and the King appointed the Earl of Lindsey. Events in Lincolnshire were affected by the position of Royalist Newark just across the border, the strategic importance of the Trent crossing there and at Gainsborough, and the dominance of Parliamentary support in East Anglia. The early success in Yorkshire by the middle of 1643 except for the port of Hull, of the Royalists under William Cavendish, Earl of Newcastle, made Lincolnshire's involvement certain. Lord Willoughby had had some success in mobilising Parliamentary support but as early as April 1643 Oliver

Cromwell, along with elements from Lincolnshire, failed to dislodge the Royalists from Newark. At the same time Lord Willoughby had more success at Gainsborough which he secured for Parliament, thus cutting off Royalist access to north Lincolnshire. This also disrupted an important communication link between Newark and Royalist York. Therefore, Gainsborough became a target and was besieged by a Royalist force under the command of Sir Charles Cavendish, a cousin of the Duke of Newcastle, but it was rescued by Parliamentary reinforcements commanded by Cromwell, and the Royalists were routed in a battle in fields to the north east of the town. However, Parliament's success was brief, for within a short time the Earl of Newcastle appeared with his army across the Trent, forcing the Parliamentary soldiers out of the town. Newcastle pursued the retreating Parliamentary forces, capturing Lincoln and Tattershall Castle without having to resort to arms. The retreat to Boston, Spalding and Peterborough was so rapid that Parliamentary troops left behind their heavy artillery. At this point Newcastle could have pressed home his advantage, and brought the entire county under Royalist control but instead he turned his attention to Parliament's enclave at Hull. The Royalists' failure to capitalise on their advantageous position proved to be a turning point, for it gave the Parliamentary forces of the Eastern Association time to reorganise under the leadership of the Earl of Manchester, who led his army back into the county via Boston and Bolingbroke. While he consolidated his position Cromwell ferried the besieged Parliamentary forces from Hull back to Boston. This newly reinforced army was now ready to move against Royalist Lindsey and soon defeated a small Royalist force attempting to consolidate defences at Wainfleet. In the meantime there was skirmishing between further Royalist forces and a Parliamentary detachment sent from Newark to relieve Bolingbroke. As Parliamentary forces moved towards Bolingbroke, the Earl of Manchester turned towards Newark. The scene was set for a major battle. The two armies, between them comprising perhaps as many as 10,000 men, met at Winceby, to the east of Horncastle, on 11 October 1643. The Parliamentary side was under the command of Cromwell, Manchester and Sir Thomas Fairfax, newly relieved from Hull, while the Royalists were led by Sir John Henderson, Governor of Newark, and Sir William Widdrington of Blankney, who had been left by Newcastle in charge of the Lincolnshire Royalists. The Battle of Winceby was intense. Beginning at midday, the Royalist Foot soon gave way under a cavalry charge. Unable to counter-attack the Royalist troops took flight. Events happened so swiftly that at the rear Manchester's Foot never engaged the enemy and had to content themselves with rounding up Royalist stragglers.

Parliament was now in the ascendancy in the county and soon reoccupied Lincoln which was taken without battle and was garrisoned by troops from the Eastern Association. Gainsborough fell shortly afterwards to forces from Hull which marked the extinction of all Royalist forces from the county except for a small enclave in the Isle of Axholme.

The King turned to Denmark for support in the hope that they would be able to land a force on the Lincolnshire coast but, because Parliament controlled the sea ways, this was not possible.

With Parliament dominant in the county, the commanders again turned their attentions to Newark. Royalists continued raids into Kesteven as far as Sleaford and Grantham, driving out livestock and skirmishing with Parliamentary forces. While a number of Royalist forces were removed from Newark to support the Earl of Newcastle at York, a Parliamentary force, consisting of many Lincolnshire men, again besieged the town. Bad weather and internal discontent amongst the Parliamentary forces delayed the start, but the siege finally began at the end of February 1644. However, the delays allowed Prince Rupert to come to the town's rescue. Rupert's army was so overwhelming that they were able to march on Lincoln and re-occupied the castle in the name of the King and they subsequently controlled much of the county. Again this was short-lived. Parliamentary forces under Manchester, who now had authority in Lincolnshire as it had been brought into the Eastern Association, and Cromwell were on their way to join with Sir Thomas Fairfax who was laying siege to York. Although Prince Rupert had to return to Oxford with a large number of his men, the Royalist forces put up a spirited, but ultimately unsuccessful defence of Lincoln against overwhelming Parliamentary forces. Their failure to surrender resulted in substantial damage to the upper part of the city. For the last time Lincoln and the county changed hands. Newark held out until May 1646, despite being ordered to surrender by the King, resulting in a series of minor incursions into Lincolnshire, but for the most part the county remained unaffected by events elsewhere.

The second Civil War, brought about by the King's alliance with the Scots and a general dissatisfaction with Parliament's 'Rump' government, hardly affected the county as most of the action occurred in the north west and the south east of the country. However, there was heightened fear of a Royalist resurgence, particularly that Newark might rise again for the Royalist cause, which led to Edward Rossiter, who had played an important role towards the end of the first Civil War, being sent to take charge of the county's defence. Royalist forces under the leadership of Sir Philip Monckton did enter Lincolnshire from Yorkshire via the Isle of Axholme and went on to Lincoln where they plundered the city, but this occupation was short-lived. Soon the Royalists were pursued down the Fosse Way and out of the county to be caught and routed by Rossiter's Parliamentary forces. These events illustrate the lack of commitment in the county for either side since Royalists did not rise to support Monckton, and Rossiter had little success in gathering together troops for Parliament.

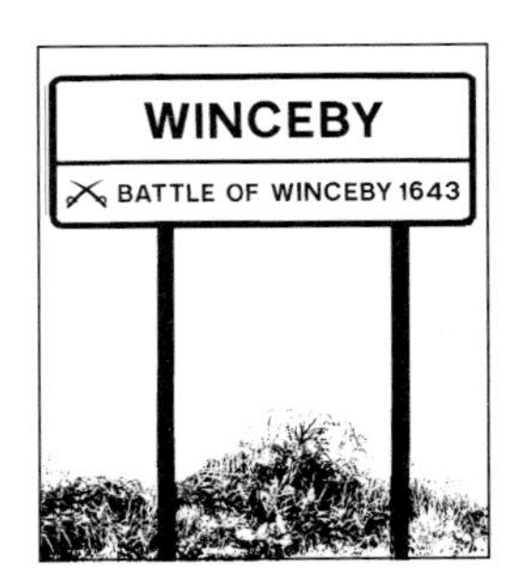

53 *Winceby.*

The end of the war meant counting the costs. The plunder of crops and livestock is part of war. In 1643, Parliamentary forces seized wool worth £2,500 from Sir Edward Hussey's store at Honington and later the same year drove off beasts worth a further £1,800. At Osgodby,

animals worth £2,000 were taken. These amounts were enormous, but many more smallholders were affected by troops from both sides as they moved through the county plundering farms and smallholdings. The gentry who had sided with the King were most affected, as their estates were sequestrated, only to be returned after the payment of fines. Many parish churches were desecrated in the name of the Puritans as Parliamentary forces traversed the county. Routinely, statues and screens were smashed and altar-rails were removed because they did not conform to the new religious ideology. Much damage was done to Lincoln Cathedral including the destruction of the medieval stained-glass windows. Once the excesses of war were over the interregnum was characterised by new government tolerance which encouraged radical religious sects. The Baptists were one such group that began to grow during the 1650s. However, The Society of Friends, the Quakers, were the most radical and outspoken during this period. George Fox came to the county in 1652 preaching his 'inner light' doctrine, speaking against formal religion and promoting an anti-authoritarian approach to religion and society in general. Quakers were certainly not prepared to bow down to earthly patronage. Edward Reynor was denounced for addressing the mayor and aldermen of Lincoln as 'right worshipful' as they were considered 'hallow deceitful, unwarrantable titles' that were the 'inventions of the beast'. Richard Farnsworth, who had led Quaker activities in the Isle of Axholme wrote to Fox in typically uncompromising terms: 'In the eternall power of God which bindeth kings in chains and princes in fetters of iron, which power shaketh kingdomes and turns the world upside down'.

Despite the often violent opposition of the fenmen to drainage schemes before the Civil War, the question was reopened in the Rump parliament, which was sympathetic to the undertakers on the grounds that improvements would be of 'great advantage to the commonwealth'. The Bedford Level Act was passed in May 1649. This gave renewed hope to the undertakers of drainage schemes in the Isle of Axholme and on the Lindsey Level. After complex and balanced legal arguments with claim and counter-claim, eventually the commoners lost out more because of their association with dissident 'Levellers' and the use of 'high, reproachful and seditious language' than to any overwhelming claims by the undertakers. The fenmen who had sided with Parliament had been betrayed.

The period of Parliamentary and army control ended with little sorrow in Lincolnshire. Higher taxes, increased centralisation of government (which had in part been causes of the original conflict), the decline in religious direction and authority, and Richard Cromwell's incompetence meant that the restoration of Charles II in 1660 was broadly welcomed. Dissatisfaction had caused some major realignments. Lord Willoughby of Parnham, who had been Parliament's commander during the first Civil War, had already changed sides in 1648 and Edward Rossiter, who represented the county in parliament at the end of the

decade, took a leading role in the negotiations with Charles' agents. Other ex-Parliamentary supporters—for example, the Kings of Ashby-de-la-Launde, the Ayscoughs of South Kelsey—and ex-Royalists—the Fanes of Fulbeck, Husseys of Caythorpe, Monsons of Carlton, Scropes of Cockerington and Thorolds of Marston—were to become major players in county affairs over the following centuries.

54 *Conflict in the Civil War.*

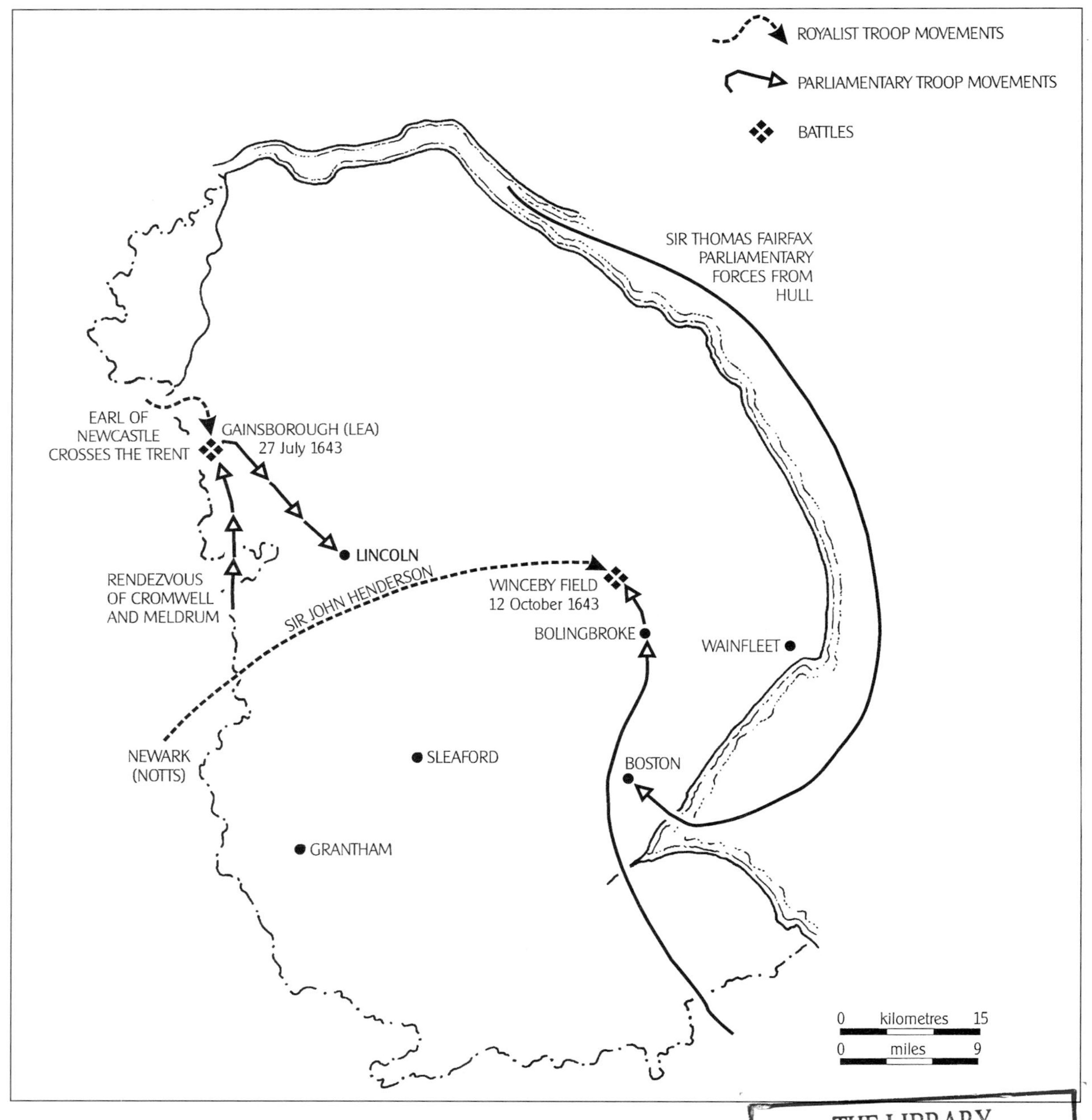

10

The Great Challenge

Political and legal difficulties caused delays in drainage schemes, but there were also severe technical problems to be overcome. Engineers were faced with difficulties on a scale which would tax their ingenuity over a number of centuries. The Isle of Axholme in the north west of the county, the Vale of Trent to the west of the Lincoln Edge and the Ancholme Valley were all subject to flooding. However, due to inundation from the sea and drainage from the land, the problem was most acute in the Fens. The Fen area is substantial, incorporating not only the south-eastern part of Lincolnshire, aptly named the Lincolnshire 'Parts of Holland', but also extensive areas of Cambridgeshire and Norfolk and less of Northamptonshire and Huntingdonshire. As with the Isle of Axholme, the Fens supported a traditional way of life, opposed to any improvements, which would radically alter the complex pattern of Fen economy, which had evolved over hundreds of years. That large areas of Fen were flooded almost every year for up to three or four months was accepted by many local people as natural and inevitable as the seasons themselves. Any attempt to implement a major strategic drainage scheme after the 17th century inevitably met with opposition.

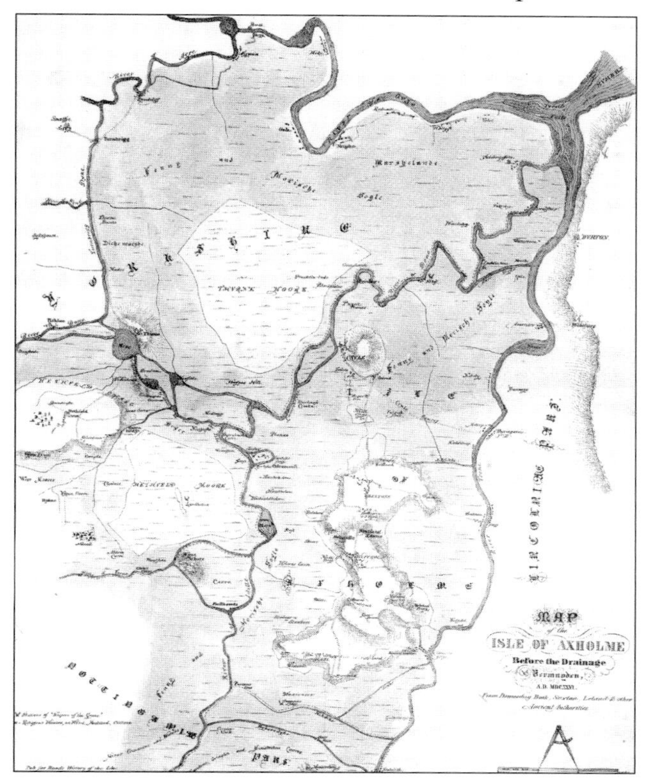

55 *The Isle of Axholme in 1624.*

The Romans had cut the Carr Dyke which, like the Fosse Dyke, was not only a navigable canal but an early attempt at large-scale drainage. The Carr Dyke joined the river Witham just east of Lincoln with the river Nene to the east of Peterborough and acted as a catch-water drain at the boundary of the Fens. This attempt at strategic planning soon fell into disrepair in the fifth century, once the Roman administration ceased. During the Middle Ages the Commission of Sewers was established with the object of over-seeing the upkeep of

embankments and the cleansing of watercourses. However, because each village was responsible for the part of the watercourse which passed through its parish, co-ordination and enforcement was almost impossible, despite the need for action. In 1531 the Commission was given real powers. It gained a strategic planning role to 'survey the said walls, streams, ditches, banks, gutters, sewers, gotes, calcies, bridges, trenches, mills, mill-dams, flood-gates, ponds, locks, hebbing wears, and other impediments, lets and annoyances'; but most importantly it had legal powers to enforce them 'to be made, corrected, repaired, amended, put down, or reformed, as the case shall require'. The Commission of Sewers with its keepers, bailiffs and surveyors remained in operation, although much amended, until the 19th century. No sooner had the Commissioners' new powers been granted than one of the unifying organisations of the Fens was destroyed. With the dissolution of the monasteries after 1536 their function as custodians and agricultural improvers including drainage also disappeared. The impact would have been enormous. For example, near the river Witham between Lincoln and the river Slea, there were 12 religious houses: Sheepwash Grange, Branston Grange, Nocton Priory, Linwood Grange, Catley Priory, Kyme Priory, Kirkstead Abbey, Stixwould Priory, Tupholme Priory, Bardney, Stainfield and Barlings Abbey and their associated lands.

56 *The peasant economy. Fen slodgers returning with their catch.*

Piecemeal improvements to the Fens were carried on throughout the 16th and into the early 17th centuries. Of these, the most important was the cutting in 1568 of the Maud Foster Drain to the north of Boston, which had an impact on the drainage of the West Fen described as 'imperfectly drained by narrow canals which intersect it for many miles'. Although imperfect, this represented real progress compared with the East Fen, described as in

> quite a state of nature, and exhibits a specimen of what the county was like before the introduction of drainage. It is a morass, intermixed with a number of lakes, from half to two or three miles in circuit, communicating with each other by narrow ready straits. They are shallow none above four or five feet deep but abound with pike, perch, ruff, bream, tench, dace, eels etc.

The drainage of the Isle of Axholme was begun by Sir Cornelius Vermuyden in 1626, but the first real attempt at large-scale drainage of the Lincolnshire Fens was in 1631, when Adventurers under the direction of Sir Anthony Thomas began to drain the East and West Fens between the river Witham and the coast in return for 1,600 acres of reclaimed land, of which 400 acres were to be given to the poor. This was an important provision as the Fens had for centuries provided sustenance to the poor. Substantial improvements were made, including the cutting of new drains in the West and Wildmore Fens, to the natural outfalls to the sea at Wainfleet and Friskney and to the river Witham at Anton's Gowt and New Gote. The Maud Foster drain was also enlarged and improved. In addition to the lands allotted to the Adventurers, the cost of upkeep was to be paid by granting the Mayor of Boston the rents of 2,500 acres

of drained land. The link between private profit, provision for the poor and future upkeep was the way forward for these large-scale drainage schemes. Other schemes were also under way at this time. The Earl of Lindsey drained a large area between Kyme Eau and the river Glen, for which he received a payment of land, and Sir Philibert Vernatti drained the Deeping and Crowland Fens in 1631 for the Earl of Bedford. Even Charles I initially had a direct hand in the plan to cut the South Forty Foot Drain, which also provided a 24-mile navigable river from Bourne to Boston. As in the Isle of Axholme, Charles' involvement was not popular, since it was seen as a threat to the vested interests of the commoners who, after a short time, destroyed the drain and buildings erected by the improvers. For generations they had made a living gathering 'reeds, fodder, thacks, turves, flaggs, hassocks, segg, fleggweed for fleggeren, collors, mattweede for churches, chambers, beddes and many other fenn commodytes of greate use in both towne and countreye'. This discontent is summed up in two verses of a longer poem printed in W. Dugdale's book *Imbanking and Drayning*.

> They'll sow both beans and oats, where never man yet thought it,
> Where men did row a boat, ere undertakers bought it:
> But, Ceres, thou, behold us now, let wild oats be their venture,
> Oh let the frogs and miry bogs destroy where they do entre.
>
> Behold the great design, which they do now determine,
> Will make our bodies pine, a prey to crows and vermine:
> For they do mean all Fens to drain, and waters overmaster,
> All must dry, and we must die, 'cause Essex calves want pasture.

To make things worse, many of those employed on these drainage schemes were, like Vernatti and Vermuyden, foreigners.

Progress during the early years of the 17th century came to an abrupt end with the onset of the Civil War and any improvements fell into neglect during this period of economic and political uncertainty. By comparison, there was great activity in the Fens south of Lincolnshire. Major improvements were going on in Norfolk and Cambridgeshire under the direction of the Duke of Bedford. After the Civil War negative attitudes to drainage were supported by the development of fundamentalist Puritanism. Not only did some think that the whole undertaking was impossible, but that it was wrong to alter God's work. Despite this, the economic importance of the entire fen region was clearly understood. In 1649 the Duke of Bedford's Act was passed, which made clear the economic objectives. They were to make the Fens:

> ... fit to bear coleseed and rapeseed in great abundance, which is of singular use to make soap and oils within this nation, to the advancement of the trade of clothing and spinning of wool, and much of it will be improved into good pasture for feeding and breeding of cattle, and of tillage to be sown with corn and grain, and for hemp and flax in great quantity, for making all sorts of linen cloth and cordage for shipping within this nation; which increases manufactures, commerce, and trading at home and abroad, will relieve the poor by setting them to work, and will many other ways rebound to the great advantage and strengthening of the nation.

Piecemeal schemes were undertaken during the latter half of the 17th century but did not take off until the 18th century when changes became a part of the much wider 'agricultural revolution'. A new problem was now apparent as the various drainage schemes began to yield results. As soon as the land began to dry out it shrank and the surface of the land began to drop. This was a particular problem in the vast peat area but not so acute in the silt zone of the 'town lands', which therefore locked in water in the inner Fen region. In practical terms, it made the natural flow of water between main channels such as the South Forty Foot Drain and the subsidiary channels impossible because they were lower. In fact, the entire Fen was sinking in relation to the level of the sea. The solution was to pump water from the lower levels into the upper drains. There may have been some kind of pumping 'Ingin' operating on the Fens as early as the middle of the 17th century, powered by horses. However, the windmill transformed drainage, not only in terms of efficiency but also in terms of Fen topography, since these relatively large machines could be seen for miles standing above the flat, featureless surrounding countryside. By the end of the 18th century some 63 windmills stood along the banks of the South Forty Foot Drain; by 1763 there were 50 windmills at work in Deeping Fen alone. Improvement in one area had a knock-on effect elsewhere, and the river Welland needed

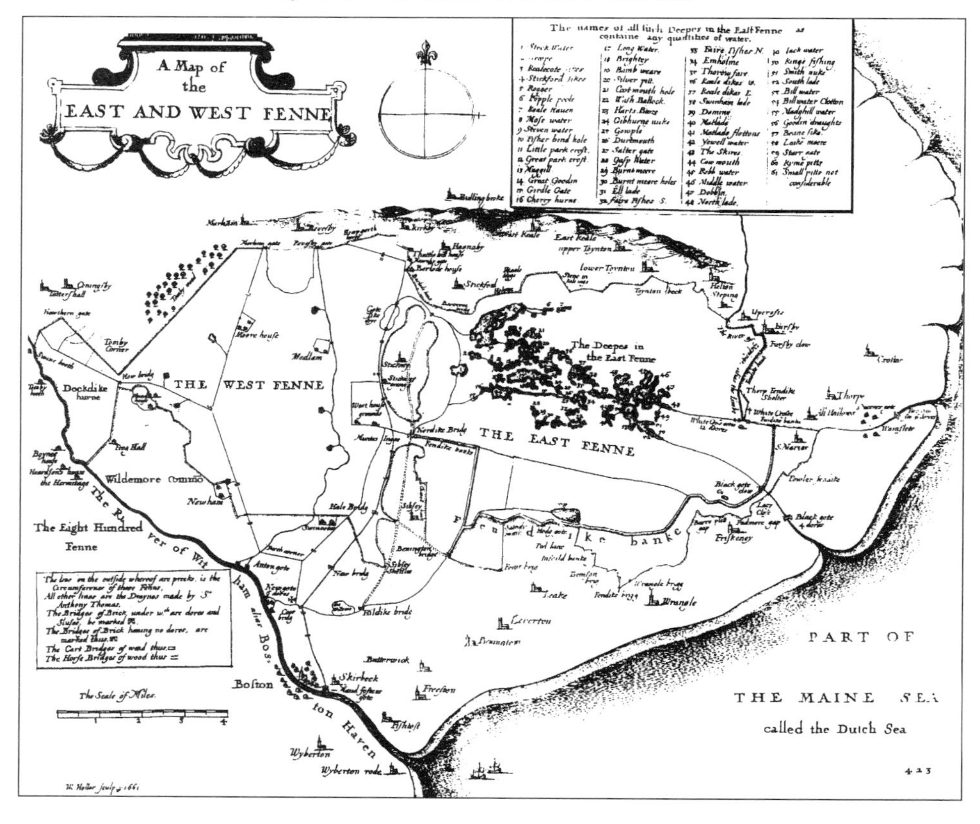

57 *William Dugdale's map of the East, West and Wildmore Fens from his book* History of Imbanking and Drayning of Divers, Fennes and Marshes *published in 1662.*

58 *Windmill drainage technology.*

to be improved. The overall effect of these improvements can be judged by the increase in land values. In 1799 Arthur Young reported, '... twenty years ago the land sold for about £3 an acre; some was then let at 7s. or 8s. an acre; and a great deal was in such a state that nobody would rent it: now it is in general worth 20s. an acre, and sells at £20 an acre'.

Although improvement was apparent, flooding was still a problem. During the winter of 1762 and the spring of 1763, 22,000 acres of Holland Fen were flooded. Subsequently the Black Sluice was built to connect the South Forty Foot Drain with the river Witham near Boston. The river Witham itself was still proving a problem. Individual proprietors had made piecemeal attempts to improve their section of the river by cutting drains, erecting mills and embanking, but the need for effective strategic action had become apparent. The fall from High Bridge at Lincoln to Boston was only 16 feet; the river was 'crooked' and as little as 18 feet wide in places. Winter usually brought flooding. The preamble to the 1762 Act made clear the situation:

> ... by the sand and silt brought in by the tide, the outfalls thereof into the sea hath, for many years last past, been greatly hindered and obstructed, and is now, in a great measure, stopped up, lost and destroyed and thereby great part of the low lands and fens lying on both sides of the said river (together about one hundred thousand acres) are frequently overflowed, and rendered useless and unprofitable, to the great loss of the respective owners thereof, the decay of trade and commerce ...

Towards the end of the 18th century land rentals along the Witham had risen from 1s.6d. per acre to between 11s. and 17s. To the east of the river Witham the problems of the Wildmore, West and East Fens remained. In 1800 it was stated, 'Of the last six seasons four have been so wet that most of the new enclosed Fens bordering on the Witham were inundated ... Many hundred acres of the harvest of 1799 were reaped by men in boats'. In 1799 John Rennie was asked by Sir Joseph Banks of Revesby Abbey, which overlooked West Fen where he leased a large area of land from the Duchy of Lancaster, to undertake surveys of Wildmore and East and West Fens. His conclusion, which appeared the following year, recognised that the main problem was the overflow of upland waters in the Fens and the poor outfalls. The work that followed was substantial. A catchwater drain was constructed from Coningsby in the west to join the Gote Syke Drain and the Maud Foster Sluice was moved and enlarged. The East Fen was serviced by a catchwater drain from Little Steeping to join the West Fen Catchwater south of Stickford. In addition, a new sluice called Hobhole Sluice was constructed down river from the Maud Foster Drain, which was fed from the Hobhole Drain extending up to Stickney, eventually allowing water to bypass Maud Foster. These advances, with the construction of numerous minor dykes and of a new river Witham channel at its outfall, had a major effect on the entire area north of Boston. In addition the new townships of Eastville, Midville, Frithville, Carrington, Westville and Thornton-le-Fen were established after 1812. These soon developed into new communities. For example, the 1821 census returns showed a

59 *Sir Joseph Banks of Revesby.*

60 *St Peter's Church, Wildmore. A new church for a new village built in 1816.*

population in Eastville (acreage 2,749) of 118, at Midville (acreage 2,619) 139, and Frithville (acreage 2,900) 272. It should not be forgotten that these enormous drainage enterprises were largely undertaken by bands of itinerant workers using manpower and the simplest of tools. Many of these 'navvies' had been the bands of canal builders during the 18th century and were to become the railway builders of the 19th century.

All this was assisted by the use of steam power as a more dependable pumping system than windmills. The situation was becoming worse as the effectiveness of drainage caused the level of the Fens to continue to drop and windmills were unable to cope. John Rennie stated in 1810: '... especially when the wet weather is succeeded by calm weather, the mill cannot work, and therefore water lies on the surface of the Fens, and does incalculable injury'. In 1852, however, we learn that 'a great number of steam engines have been successively erected in almost all part of the Great Level; being most frequent in the Southern division of the Bedford Level, and in the Witham Fens towards Lincoln'. They were fast replacing windmills, being far more reliable and powerful and having the capacity to '...lift water from 6 to 16 or even 20 feet'. Red brick buildings and tall chimneys became a new feature of the flat landscape as windmills were replaced.

The major impact of drainage was on the Fens, but marshland reclamation of the coastal strip should not be forgotten. Attempts were made during the medieval period to safeguard the coastline from inundation from the sea with the construction of clay banks; and also in the 17th century when over 17,000 acres was saved from the sea along the coast principally south of the river Welland. The main impetus to recover the marshes came at times of high prosperity. Such a time occurred during

the French Wars of 1793-1815 when 4,595 acres of marshlands were embanked in Spalding, Moulton, Whaplode, Holbeach and Gedney and a further 700 acres between Frieston and Friskney. Throughout the 19th century nearly all Fen coastal parishes were enlarged by new land reclaimed from the marsh, even to the extent that a completely new 3,193-acre parish of Central Wingland was created.

The great undertakings of Fen drainage had been completed by the beginning of the 20th century. All the main drainage schemes were in place and work during the 20th century has on the whole involved maintenance and improvement, rather than new constructions within the Fens. Steam pumping engines were replaced by even more powerful diesel or electric engines and embankments have been strengthened, channels constantly dredged and river outfalls improved. Further north along the coast there have been some improvements to the coastal defences in response to the growing number of holidaymakers and because money was being invested in the hinterland in buildings and good quality agricultural land. At Skegness a sea wall was built in 1878 and at Cleethorpes in 1902. Since the 1860s attempts have been made to halt the natural movement of beaches southwards by constructing groynes along stretches of the coast. Lengths of concrete defences were built by the 1940s at Trusthorpe, Sutton, Sandilands, Chapel St Leonards and Ingoldmells. These measures combined with natural sand-dunes along a great length of the coast provided the main sea defence.

Lincolnshire's coast is fragile. Over the centuries much has changed. For example the medieval churches at Mablethorpe St Peter, Trusthorpe, Sutton and Mumby have disappeared into the sea and the coastline only survives in its current state because of increased human intervention to prevent inundation by the sea of the low-lying outer and inner marsh and Fens. By the beginning of the 20th century, despite the investment which had taken place in the Fens, the rest of the coast depended mainly on inadequate clay or sand banks. By the end of the Second World War there had been some improvement to some sections by the use of concrete. The entire sea defence system was found wanting in 1953 as a result of a storm surge which breached most of the coast from north of Immingham to

61 *The title page of the Act of Parliament for draining the East, West and Wildmore Fens, 1801.*

ANNO QUADRAGESIMO PRIMO

GEORGII III. REGIS.

Cap. 135.

An Act for the better and more effectually draining certain Tracts of Land, called *Wildmore Fen*, and *The West* and *East Fens*, in the County of *Lincoln*, and alſo the Low Lands and Grounds in the ſeveral Pariſhes, Townſhips, and Places having Right of Common on the ſaid Fens, and other Low Lands and Grounds lying contiguous or adjoining thereto. [2d *July* 1801.]

WHEREAS there are certain Tracts of Land called *Wildmore Fen*, and *The West and East Fens* in the County of *Lincoln*, containing together Forty thouſand Acres or thereabouts: And whereas by an Act, paſſed in the Second Year of the Reign of His preſent Majeſty, intituled, *An Act for draining and preſerving certain Low Lands, called* The Fens, *lying on both Sides of the River* Witham, *in the County of* Lincoln, *and for reſtoring and maintaining the Navigation of the ſaid River from the High Bridge in the City of* Lincoln, *through the Borough of* Boſton, *to the Sea*, it was enacted, that the Low Lands and Fens therein-after mentioned and deſcribed, ſhould be drained and improved by, with, and under ſuch Powers and Authorities, and ſubject to ſuch Rules, Orders, Directions, and Proviſions, and by ſuch Ways and Means as were therein-after directed and preſcribed; and it was thereby further enacted and declared, that the ſame Low Lands and Fens ſhould be deemed to conſiſt of and be divided into Six ſeveral Diſtricts or Diviſions to be reſpectively

[*Loc. & Per.*] 23 Z

62 *Pinchbeck pumping station built in 1833 to improve the drainage of Spalding and Pinchbeck.*

Gibraltar Point south of Skegness and inundated a large inland area. This was a major disaster not only in financial terms, but in human terms, for it claimed 41 lives. Since 1953, there has been a gradual improvement to the sea defences along the entire coast, made even more imperative by the increasing investment in the flood risk area. At the end of the 20th century more than 35,000 people live behind the sea defences between Mablethorpe and Skegness. In recent years, under the strategic planning of the National Rivers Authority, sea walls have been improved and a process of 'beach nourishment' has been undertaken, whereby sand is pumped ashore to raise the level of the beach. Whatever method is used, the coast will still face the forces of nature in the future. The sea walls and banks will continue to be eroded, the long-shore drift of sand and gravel will continue to change the coastline, altering the beaches and dunes which provide protection, and the eastern side of Britain will continue to sink into the North Sea. Changing weather patterns, which are likely to produce more surges of the type in 1953, and the impact of rising sea levels as a result of global warming will mean that the pressure on the defence of the Lincolnshire coast will only increase.

11

Agricultural Change 1750-1850

When Arthur Young, the observer and writer about agriculture, was describing the changes in farming in his two books published in 1799 and 1813 relating to Lincolnshire, this was at a time of fundamental developments which were to have far-reaching effects. As with Young, no one at the time could have failed to see the momentous changes to the landscape and to farming methods and working practices, which over a relatively short period of time affected nearly every Lincolnshire parish and most of the population. The social ramifications of these physical changes were more subtle but, nevertheless, as real. Different attitudes and relationships developed as farmers became orientated towards profit and loss and less paternalistic, described by James Obelkevich, in his account of change in Lindsey, as 'From Community to Class Society'. The term 'Agricultural Revolution' is entirely correct when applied to Lincolnshire, as the changes occurred quickly, were fundamental and long lasting, and they reinforced the county's pre-eminent position as an agricultural economy which has lasted until the 21st century.

63 *Labourers' housing. Mud and stud cottage at Thimbleby—much restored.*

Enclosure of parishes was the most fundamental change in agriculture because it enabled new farming methods to be adopted by allowing farmers to invest often considerable amounts of money in land which they owned to reap the benefits in higher profits or from higher rents. Although enclosure was most common from 1760, some had already taken place. During the 16th and 17th centuries, some parishes had been enclosed and others partially enclosed at the behest of individual landowners. This was usually common land, an area of the parish particularly important to the poor. The aim of these early enclosures was often to increase pasture at the expense of arable land. This process also had social consequences leading to the depopulation of some parishes and an increase in vagrancy, much to the concern of Elizabeth I's government. By the middle of the 18th century enclosure could take place in two ways, by private agreement or by Act of Parliament. Just over 40 per cent of Lincolnshire parishes were privately enclosed either by agreement between landowners or more often where the parish was 'closed', i.e., controlled by a single or very few owners. Of 45 parishes which were owned by a single proprietor (based on 1831 land ownership figures) only six were not enclosed privately. Most private enclosure was undertaken relatively quickly, but this was not always the case. The parish of Cleatham took from 1624 to 1710 to enclose and Holton-le-Moor was enclosed in two parts. The western part of the parish was enclosed by the middle of the 17th century and the eastern 'moor' by the middle of the 19th century. Both parishes were in the hands of single proprietors.

Regional variations are apparent. Some 63 per cent of Lindsey parishes and 52 per cent of Kesteven parishes were privately enclosed compared with only 31 per cent of the parishes in Holland. In 'closed' parishes dominant landowners had the power to promote enclosure and indeed had most to gain. In such parishes rents could be increased on completion as crop yields went up. Conversely, in the multi-proprietor 'open' parishes enclosure was usually authorised by an Act of Parliament. Enclosure in the large 'open' parishes of the Isle of Axholme, north coastal parishes and almost all the Fen parishes was subject to parliamentary permission.

The amount of enclosure activity (15 Acts) during the earlier periods pales into insignificance compared with the 60 years after 1760 when there were 310 Enclosure Acts. The table below shows the number of Lincolnshire Acts to affect the county to 1836. After a period between 1760-79 when a large number of Acts was passed due to new demand for agricultural produce encouraged by a steady rise in the nation's population, the growth of new cities and the improved transport provided by canals, there was a substantial decline only to build up again between 1790-1819. This second increase was a period of particularly high profits for farmers when, for example, the price of wheat rose from between 60s. and 80s. per quarter to 120s. per quarter, brought about by the Napoleonic Wars between 1793 and 1815.

Lincolnshire Enclosure Acts to 1836

	Acts of Parliament passed for parishes in			
	Lindsey	Kesteven	Holland	% of total
Before 1760	8	7	0	4.9
1760-1769	30	16	3	15.8
1770-1779	46	22	9	24.9
1780-1789	4	7	3	4.5
1790-1799	28	21	5	17.5
1800-1809	34	19	4	18.5
1810-1819	18	8	9	11.4
1820-1829	4	1	0	1.6
1830-1836	2	1	0	0.9

After the passing of the Enclosure Acts the subsequent awards and surveys, drawn up under the direction of three Commissioners appointed by parliament, provide an enormous amount of detail. Not only did they allocate land to those who had title to land before the Act, but they allocated land in lieu of the unpopular tithes and other ancient property rights. At Waltham, for example, the rector received 327 acres, and Luck and Joseph Anningson, the principal landowners in the parish, were allotted 22 acres in lieu of manorial rights in addition to 732 acres from the general allotment. Forty-seven acres was even allotted to the parish church of St John's in Newport, Lincoln and 24 acres to the parish church of Aylesbury, Buckinghamshire. New roads and wide verges, bordered by new hedges, were made and ditches were dug for drainage. In Lincolnshire today, wide verges along country lanes are common. At Waltham six new 60 ft. wide public roads were planned for access to the new farms which were to be built. One major change brought about by the new allocation of land was the breakdown of the traditional nucleated village. Instead farms and farm buildings were now built on the newly acquired land. Parishes acquired new substantial houses and their associated assortment of farm buildings on their now legally secure holdings. In addition to public roads, they also established footpaths, bridleways and drains. The Commissioners wanted to establish the new boundaries as quickly and permanently as possible, so they ordered that the fences between the allotments should be planted with 'quicksets and guarded by posts and two high rails' within a year of the Award. Being an Enclosure Commissioner became for some almost a career. John Grantham of Stallingborough, one of the three Commissioners for the Waltham enclosure, also worked on the enclosures of Keelby, Wootton and Barnoldby le Beck and, whilst working on the Waltham enclosure, he also implemented those at Scawby, Atterby, Snitterby, Waddingham and Winterton. This tally was low compared with John Burcham of Coningsby, who between 1801 and 1846 was Commissioner on at least 70 enclosures mostly in Lincolnshire but also in Rutland, Leicestershire, Huntingdonshire and Nottinghamshire.

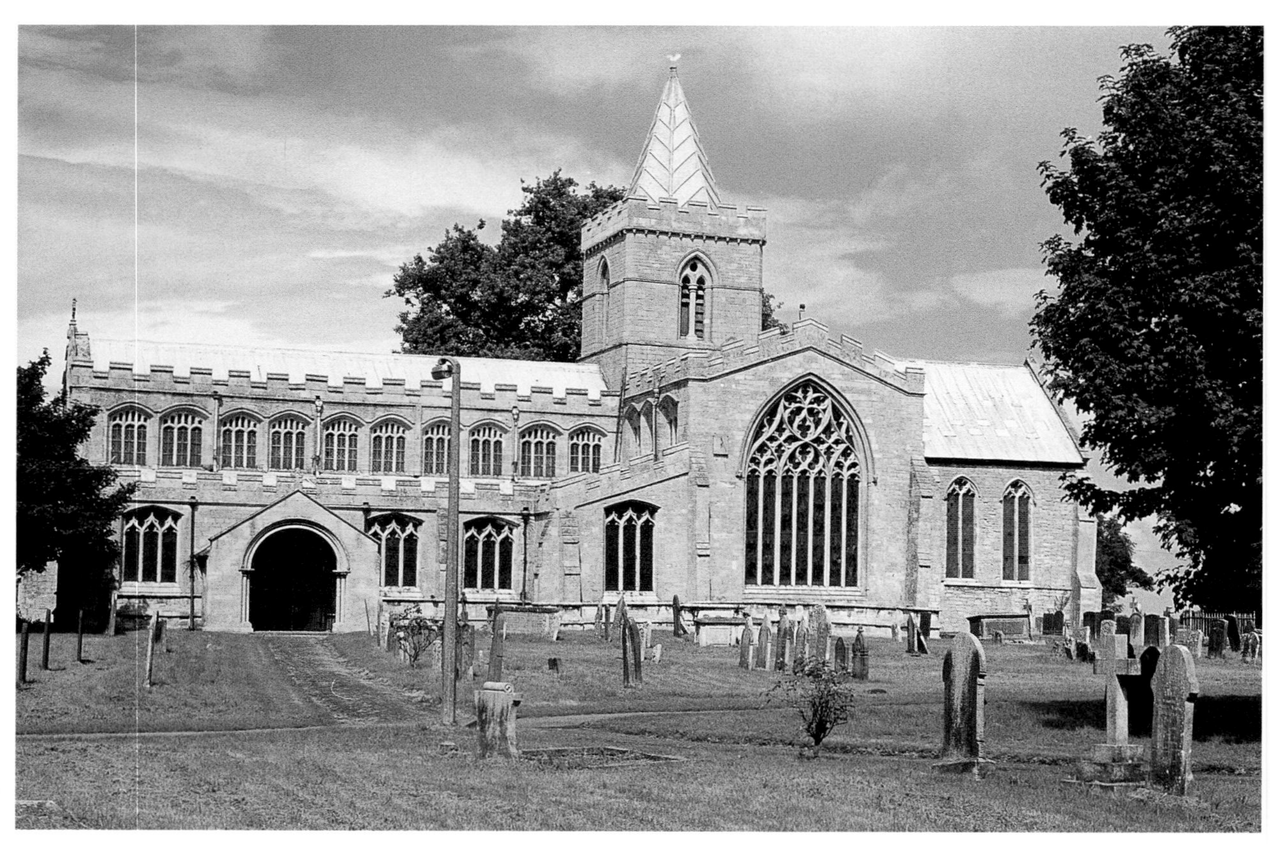

VI *St Peter and St Paul's Church, Algarkirk was built in the 13th century.*

VII *Crowland Abbey.*

VIII *Boothby Pagnell Manor House built about 1200.*

IX *Estate housing at Blankney built in the 1830s-40s.*

The costs involved in general enclosure and parliamentary enclosure in particular were enormous, and it was the buoyant economic state of the market and the prospect of receiving a high return which encouraged the enclosure of many parishes. Even so, not all parishes were quick to enclose. Discussions at North Thoresby first took place in 1801 and three more times before the parish was eventually enclosed in 1846. At North Kelsey the farmers were watching the increasing agricultural prices between 1795, when enclosure was first discussed, until 1812 when agreement was finally reached. Some parishes were prevented by outside interests from proceeding. At Wrawby, for example, there was a move by the main owners to enclose in 1794, but they were prevented by Clare College, Cambridge, who were unhappy with some of the terms. Agreement was not reached until 1800. At Sleaford and Quarrington the opposite applied, as the enclosure was instigated by the Earl of Bristol, the absentee owner of most of the soil. An Act covering both village and town was obtained in 1794. It cost £5,267 16s. 0d. (£5,267.80) or £1 4s. 4d. per acre (£1.22) to enclose Kirton Lindsey between 1793 and 1801; £8,243 2s. 3d. (£8,243.11) or £1.18s.11d. per acre (£1.95) for Hibaldstow between 1796 and 1803 and Wrawby-cum-Brigg, £4,950 2s. 10d. (£4,950.14) or £1 13s. 3d. per acre (£1.66) between 1800 and 1805. In this last example, the sum of £968 was spent on legal and parliamentary fees associated with obtaining the Act, surveyor's fees accounted for £566, road making, drainage and constructing bridges accounted for a further £1,202, fencing £1,207, and the fees for the three Commissioners appointed by the Act, £806. Not surprisingly, the greatest costs fell on the largest landowner, often the instigators, but with potentially the most to gain. In the case of Wrawby, Robert Carey Elwes Esq received 1,372 acres and paid just over £3,061 compared with Christopher Richardson who received just over one-sixth of an acre and paid just 5s. For the large owner some of

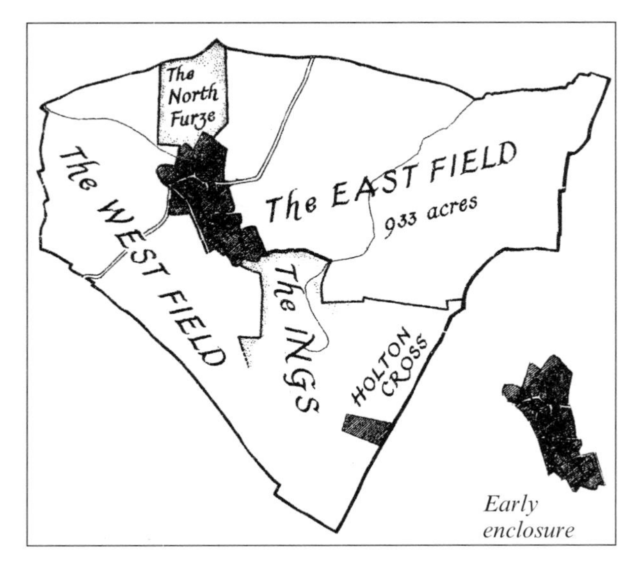

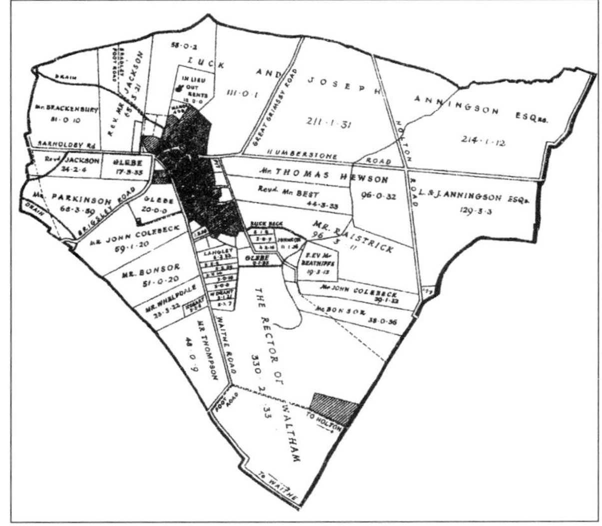

64 *The parish of Waltham before and after enclosure.*

these costs could be recovered from higher rents through the increased production made possible by enclosure. Despite the costs involved, there was no overall decrease in the numbers of smaller proprietors during the period of high agricultural prices brought about by the French Wars. Nor did it cause major rural depopulation in the short term as there was much work involved in the enclosing process and the increased production that it encouraged. In addition, for the first half of the 19th century there was no major industry to provided alternative employment in the county.

Arthur Young was right in 1813 when he wrote in *A General view of the Agriculture of Lincolnshire*,

> ... in attempting to give a general view of the soil of this very extensive county, I must promise that not one can be named which contains a greater variety; for it may truly be said to include all sorts of land that are to found in the kingdom...1. clays, 2. sand, 3. loam, 4. chalk, 5. peat; they are all to be found in many districts, under many variations.

A general picture of the crops grown in the county at the beginning of the 19th century can be gained from the 1801 Crop Returns collected as part of a government survey. The survey was not mandatory, yet 78 per cent of Lincolnshire parishes sent in a return, so this provides a representative sample of arable farming in the county. Barley was the dominant crop followed closely by wheat and oats and then by relatively small acreages of rye grass and potatoes. Although barley was the most important crop overall, there were regional differences. Wheat was the most important crop in the north west in the Isle of Axholme, the lower Trent Vale and along the low-lying north-eastern coastal marsh. In the parishes of the eastern Wolds turnip/rape (not separated in the returns), oats and barley dominated, whilst in the fens oats were cultivated, except in the area around Deeping St James where barley dominated. The parishes of the lighter and well-drained lands of the Heath concentrated on wheat, barley and turnips/rape in almost equal proportions. Generalisations are difficult to make because even within single parishes there was often geological diversity which resulted in different crops in almost equal proportions. For example, the line of parishes straddling the Lincoln Cliff south of Harmston contains two main soils. On the eastern side there are the lighter soils of limestone Heath, suitable for cultivating barley; on the western side lay the heavy clays on which even today with all the modern drainage techniques, water lies after heavy rain, so this tended to be permanent grass for grazing. A further example is found in most of the parishes in a line northwards form Market Deeping to Heighington, which straddled the well-drained limestone of the eastern Heath and the Kesteven Uplands and the low-lying fens.

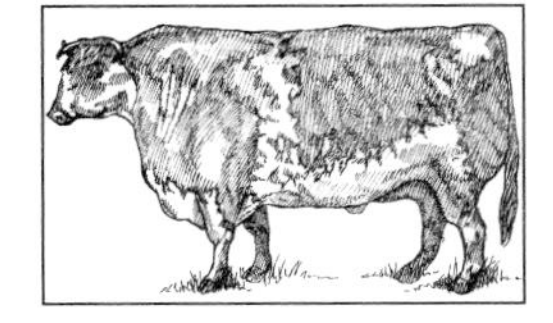

65 *Short horned bull 'Patriot', 1810.*

One important agricultural activity not included in the 1801 Survey was livestock farming. The survey did not ask for the proportion of grassland and pasture in parishes, but it was a substantial amount. In the Fens, where Arthur Young described the grazing lands as the 'glory of Lincolnshire', only 21 per cent of the total land was given over to

arable farming. However, it would be wrong to think that the rest was grassland and pasture, as the total figure included villages, towns, woodland, commons, fallow land and 'waste'. Even the most productive arable area of the Wolds had only 25.6 per cent dedicated to arable production. However, grassland and pasture constituted a considerable proportion of land, where cattle and pigs as well as poultry, horses and rabbits were produced. Sheep still dominated. They were extensively bred on the Wolds, and then sent for fattening to the pastures of the Outer Marshes. Sheep bred on the Heath and Cliff were fattened on the Fens to be sold at major sheep fairs at Caistor, Lincoln and Boston. Young was clearly surprised by the number of sheep in his 1813 description, stating that the 'information I should receive under this head [*sic*] would be considerable'. Sheep retained much of the importance in the rural economy they had had during the Middle Ages, although by the 1830s on a national scale wool was losing out to imported cotton. The demand for a dual purpose animal, one with a good quality wool and meat, grew throughout the century. Much experimentation in selective cross-breeding was undertaken with varying degrees of success until the 1870s when Henry Dudding of Riby produced the Improved Lincoln sheep. When crossed with the Merino sheep, the breed found itself as far away as South America, Australia and New Zealand, providing a good quantity of both wool and mutton. At the beginning of the 20th century there were over a million sheep in the county and it is only later in the century that there has been a dramatic decline in the sheep population. Lincoln Red Shorthorn cattle developed from a herd founded at the end of the 18th century by Thomas Turnell of Reasby. Although important it gained neither a national nor an international reputation. By the end of the 19th century horse breeding was a shadow of its former importance. In the 1830s the great Horncastle fair had been the largest in the country, attracting buyers from Europe and as far away as the USA.

66 *Excessive claims for selective breeding.*

As the agricultural industry developed a more business-like ethos, new investment had to be found for enclosure as for other undertakings such as drainage, waterway and canal improvements, and turnpike roads. To meet this demand, banks were established in Lincoln, Boston, Stamford and all market towns by the middle of the 19th century. The first bank in the county was established in 1754 by a Boston merchant, William Garfit. A reflection of the port's commercial vitality at this time is that by 1790 there were four banks there and, by 1815, a further two had been opened, which meant that Boston had more banks than anywhere else in the county. During the agricultural boom period of the 1790s to 1810s new banks were established throughout the county, being opened at Lincoln (though the first bank there was opened in 1775), Spilsby, Holbeach, Grantham, Gainsborough, Stamford and Sleaford; not all survived. Banking was a precarious business. However, it was the confidence engendered by the county's agricultural economy that encouraged banks to be established, and some to be successful.

67 *Boston May sheep fair in the early 19th century.*

Wheat prices rose to a high of 120s. per quarter during the French Wars. At the end of the war almost immediately prices dropped dramatically to below 80s. despite the Corn Laws, and then gradually fell below this. Rents in many parishes had been set in better times. For example, Jarvis' tenants at Doddington petitioned him for a reduction of their rents, complaining that they had been based on the value of corn in 1811. This produced a rent per acre figure of 16s. 9d. (84p) compared with a demand for 6s. 8d. (33p) to take into account their reduced circumstances. Jarvis' reply was sympathetic: 'I do not see how this can be avoided'. Jarvis saw the reason for it, when he said,

> ... the price of wheat is so much lower than the most thorough going enthusiant (sic) for its reduction could have brought himself to believe in his wildest speculations at the close of the French war ... We can now scarcely get what was supposed to be the lowest price at which it could be imported, and are still forced to throw the market open in order to import it lower from countries not paying out Taxes or Poor Rate.

Other landlords were equally sympathetic. Sir John Thorold, on his Syston and Marston estates, was prepared to accept a high level of tenant debt for most of the 1830s, and Thomas Syson, the land agent for Sir Gilbert Heathcote, principle landowner in and around Folkingham, suggested that he should 'let the tenants pay what they are able this time'.

The general effects of enclosure were to rationalise the piecemeal enclosure of many villages and thus to bring under cultivation a great deal of waste and common land. This enabled new methods of farming to be introduced into all parishes and not only into those with innovative farmers. Over a longer period enclosure was a requisite for changes in farming which were to enable a vast increase in agricultural production during the 'golden age of farming' of the mid-19th century.

12

Roads, Rivers and Canals

Trade was important to medieval Lincolnshire, but communication was difficult. In 1319 it had taken two parties of scholars, travelling through the county from Cambridge to York, five and nine days respectively to make the 151-mile journey. The first group travelled entirely by wagon but a second larger group travelled by road and water. It took them one day to travel between Spalding and Boston on horseback, two days in a 'great' boat between Boston and Lincoln, and one day along the Fosse Dyke to Torksey. Rivers, and especially the river Witham with its Fosse Dyke connection to the river Trent, were the main routes for trade of their time, but the speed of transportation along them reflects the slow pace of economic and commercial life. Communication by road was extremely difficult and remained so throughout the Middle Ages. The only reasonable roads were those left by the Romans although, as they had been neglected for over 700 years, they had fallen into disrepair. Rivers were mostly navigable all year round, but roads were liable to floods in the winter only to dry out, causing deep ruts, in the summer. As much of the county was low-lying, travel in the Fens and marsh during winter months was at best difficult, and often impossible.

The level of passing trade through the county declined from the 14th century, as the centres of trading activity moved first southwards and then to western counties, whose ports faced the New World. Thus the economic imperative for maintaining and improving the transport system for commercial reasons was lost. This decline in trade and the natural barriers of the Wash and the river Humber estuary meant that from the Middle Ages onwards people travelled to Lincolnshire, rather than through it. The growing importance of the Great North Road, skirting the extreme west of the county, underlined Lincolnshire's relative isolation.

By the middle of the 18th century Britain was on the verge of the industrial revolution. Lincolnshire lacked fast-flowing streams for water power and coal for steam engines, but farmers were to provide for the enormous growth in population, most of whom would be living in urban centres by the middle of the 19th century. The need to distribute food provided the impetus for transport improvements from the middle of the 18th century. Both the enclosure of parishes and the establishment of turnpikes by Act of Parliament improved the condition of the county's roads. Enclosures were widespread by the first quarter of the 19th century,

68 *Turnpike gate.*

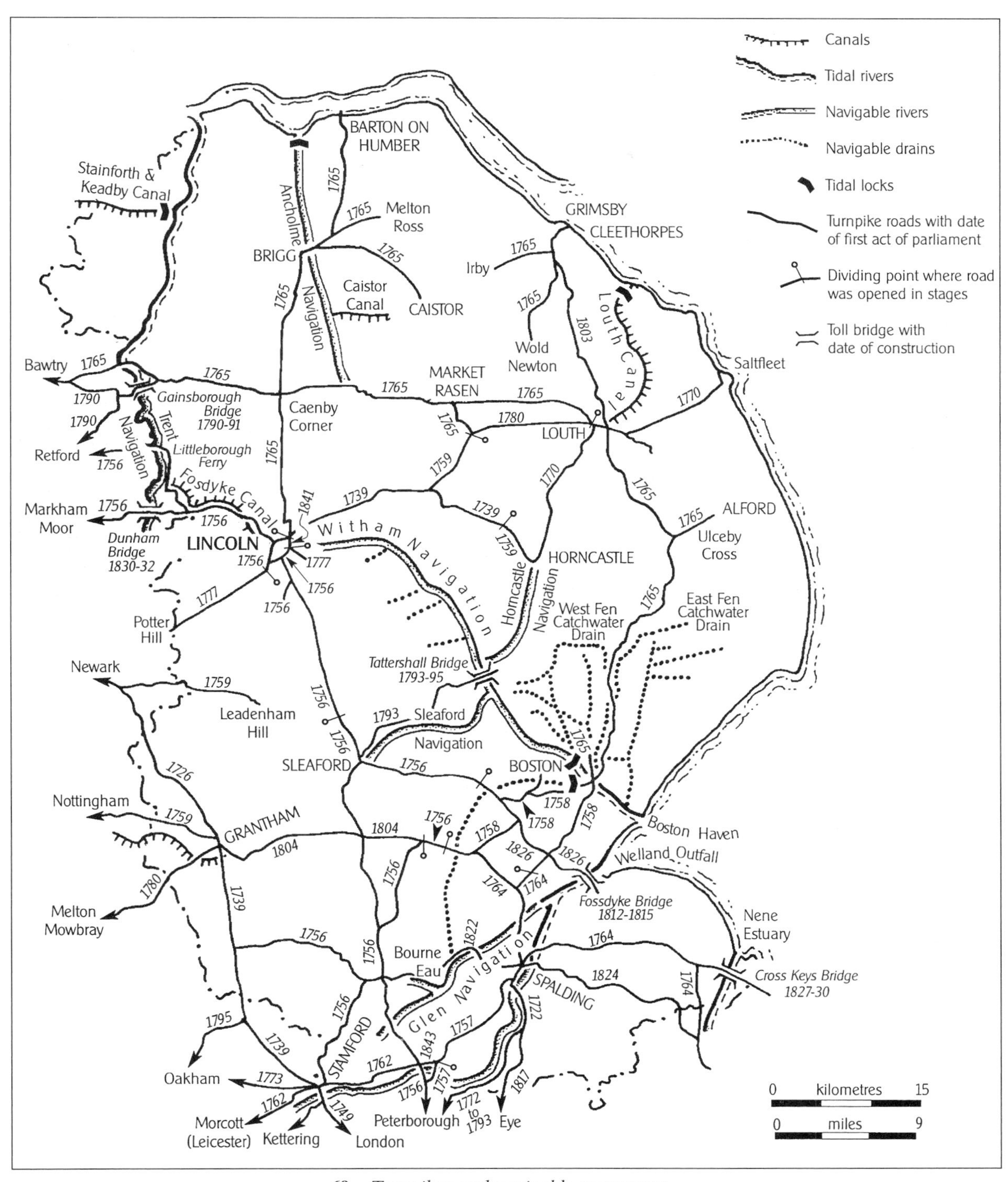

69 *Turnpikes and navigable waterways.*

70 *Toll house at Hallington on the Louth to Horncastle Turnpike.*

and thus their impact was probably greater than that of turnpikes. Many enclosure awards included land set aside for stone pits or quarries to facilitate road improvements. Even before enclosure, parish authorities elected a Surveyor of the Highways who was responsible for directing 'statute' labour. By the beginning of the 19th century work on road improvement was commonly provided as outdoor relief for the able-bodied poor. Work could always be found, and a large proportion of the total parish poor rates was devoted to it. At Billinghay, for example, of the total parish expenditure of £579 1s. 10d. (£579. 09) for the year up to March 1829, £89 6s. 10d. (£89.34) was spent on roads, of which £50 was for employing surplus labour. There was general improvement in the standard of the county's roads, but such a system relied too heavily on parishes. It was too easy for parish authorities to neglect their duties and to try to reduce the poor rates by not employing their poor. A better solution had to be sought. Major improvements were achieved by the introduction of Turnpike Trusts, which were given authority to take over sections of roads, improve them and charge a toll to travellers, coaches and herds of animals. This income paid for road upkeep and repair. Turnpikes were piecemeal but they provided better communications over long stretches of highways. The scheme was usually supported by local landed interests, who were keen to increase profits at a time of rising prices due to the improved farming methods made possible by enclosure. The connection is clear. As land became more productive and markets

were brought closer, landowners were able to increase the rents of their tenant farmers.

By the mid-1830s there were 29 Turnpike Trusts controlling 550 miles of Lincolnshire roads, though not perhaps to everyone's satisfaction. In 1826 Lord Yarborough wrote to the Lincoln-Brigg-Barton-on-Humber Trust:

> This very northern part of the county has been so accustomed to bad roads that they have scarcely a knowledge of what good roads really are. After this rain [early November 1826], new mended roads must be attended to during the Winter, and when all England is so alive to making and mending Roads do not let us get behind, indeed I consider good roads the making of a County—and I am sure they have been bad enough in this neighbourhood a length of time.

71 *The 30 metres high inland light-house, Dunston Pillar, built in 1751.*

The first turnpike road to reach Lincolnshire was the Great North Road, from Grantham northwards in 1726. The section between Grantham and Stamford was improved under an Act of 1739. The first Act of Parliament to affect a road totally within the county was passed in 1739 and provided for a turnpike between Lincoln and Baumber. However, most Acts were passed during the decade after 1756, allowing the main market towns to be connected, and thereby the foundations of the modern main road system were laid. By 1765 all the county's market towns had turnpike connections. This led to a general improvement in the county's road system, although it was still dependent on the effectiveness of the trustees and on competing interests. The profitability of the Lincoln-Brigg-Barton-on-Humber turnpike, for example, was diminished both by trade along the improved river Ancholme and the general slump in farming which affected most Trusts at the end of the Napoleonic Wars.

These improvements enabled coaching to develop. However, coaches were small, only able to carry four passengers inside and up to ten outside, and were relatively expensive. Fares on the first coaches from Lincoln to London, which began in 1784, were £1 11s. 6d. (£1.57) inside and 15s. 9d. (78p) outside, putting the trip out of the reach of the majority. Improvements to the Great North Road meant that the journey

72 *The* Greyhound *at Folkingham.*

between Edinburgh and London could be undertaken in four days, and the Stamford to London leg in one day. In 1830, at the height of the coaching era, some 70 mail and stage coaches passed through Stamford each day. Mail coaches had began in 1801, the route from London continuing from Peterborough through Sleaford to Lincoln, later extended to Hull via the Barton-on-Humber ferry. Mail coaches also soon operated from Boston to Louth. By 1830 an entire network of stage and mail coaches had developed, including some cross country to Nottingham and Manchester. The greater movement of people and mail required inns to be improved and new ones to be built. There were improved inns in main centres, such as the *George Inn* at Stamford and at Grantham and the *Peacock Inn* at Boston, which would also cater for local trade, while others were built specifically for the coach trade, such as the aptly named *Greyhound*, which dominates the wide open centre of Folkingham on the main route from London to Lincoln.

Each town had its carriers, who operated regular deliveries of all manner of goods to the surrounding area. In 1856, for example, five carriers operated from Caistor: to Brigg on Thursday, Grimsby on Friday, Louth on Wednesday and Market Rasen on Tuesday and Thursday. Even smaller villages, such as Pickworth, had one carrier operating to Grantham. The spread of railways provided a boost for carriers, as more goods were transported to station depots for local distribution. The demise of the long-distance coach was brought about by the railways, yet many turnpikes remained in operation until after 1888, when they were taken over by the new County Councils, although by this time most were struggling to survive.

73 The Angel Hotel *on the Great North Road, Grantham, 1832.*

The 20th century has seen a revolution in communication by roads and, indeed, in the quality of roads themselves. Before the era of mass car ownership, the motor bus became an important means of local transport. For the first time, people could live some distance from their place of work. Improvements to road surfaces and the flexibility offered by road vehicles offered direct competition to the railways between urban centres and many rural villages. Bus companies were often small-scale undertakings. Grimsby, at the centre of a large urban population, operated a number of services to surrounding villages from 1906. The first of these was to Caistor, a route not connected by railway, but subsequent routes included Skegness, Woodhall Spa, Louth and North Somercotes. Other local operations soon followed. Appleby's, who at the beginning of the 21st century are the largest independent coach operator in Lincolnshire, began from Conisholme near Louth in 1913. Barton's, who began a service in Mablethorpe as early as 1900 competed directly with rail when they moved to Nottingham and advertised services to the coast. By 1927 the Enterprise & Silver Dawn was operating from Scunthorpe over much of northern Lincolnshire. In the following year the Silver Queen Company, which had been established at Lincoln in 1922, was renamed the Lincolnshire Road Car Company and eventually came to dominate the entire county. Bus services allowed development beyond the railway station. It is unlikely that Billy Butlin would have built his first Holiday Camp at Ingoldmells in 1936, a few miles north of Skegness, without the availability of bus transport for the thousands of campers arriving at Skegness station on a Saturday morning.

Lincolnshire's waterways remained at varying levels of activity throughout the Middle Ages. As with the roads, the impetus for major development and expansion was brought about by the growing demand for agricultural produce and the availability of finance during the 18th century. Early improvements were almost entirely funded by local farming interests but later, because of the development of a national network, a number of schemes were supported by out-of-county interests. Lincolnshire can boast the first canal in Britain in the Roman Fosse Dyke. However, improvements to water transport chiefly involved rivers, which are thus termed 'navigations', as distinct from building new canals.

74 *Appleby's luxury in the early 1950s.*

The first undertaking in modern times to improve a waterway was done under the authority of the Act passed in 1570 'for making the River Welland ... navigable from Stamford to the Sea'. When the navigation was eventually completed, between 1664 and 1673, it was the longest locked waterway in the country. The main period of waterway improvement occurred between 1760 and 1830 when a number of Acts of Parliament were passed for the Witham Navigation, the Bourne Eau Navigation, the Glen Navigation, the Ancholme Navigation, the Sleaford Navigation which was an improvement to the river Slea, and the Horncastle Navigation, which was an improvement to the river Bain and flowed, as did the river Slea, into the river Witham. The Louth Canal was an improvement to part of the river Ludd.

Of these projects the first was the Louth Canal from the Wolds town of Louth to the coast at Tetney, a distance of less than 12 miles. Before it opened, imports of coal, timber and other commodities and exports of wool and corn had to be transported by road to the coast at Saltfleetby, Tetney and Grimsby. The feasibility enquiry by Spalding engineer, John Grundy, in 1756 states clearly the impetus for the canal which was to apply to all such undertakings. This highlighted the difficulty and expense of land carriage which is 'effected to the great hurt and detriment of Trade and Commerce and to the great hurt and disadvantage of the Landed Interests of all the country adjoining'. Despite the urgency stated in the report, the Act of Parliament giving authority to build the canal was not passed until 1763, after a further report by John Smeaton. Even so, the canal was not finally opened until 1770 at a total cost of £27,500. To reach Louth eight locks had to be constructed up the eastern slope of the Wolds with a tidal lock at Tetney into the mouth of the Humber.

75 *The disused Louth Canal at Alvingham.*

Unlike the Louth scheme, the decision to make the Ancholme navigable was based on the need for improved drainage. Great improvements were made to the river after 1635 when Sir John Monson was given authority to improve drainage, and the river was straightened, taking on its modern form. Without constant upkeep, the river fell into disrepair and in 1767 a new Act was passed to improve both drainage and navigation. Drainage was the dominant motive for improvement, although the commercial potential soon became apparent. As with the

76 *The Humber Keel was used on the county's waterways.*

Louth scheme, the Ancholme was tidal and required a lock which was built at Ferriby. Improvements to the river Glen and the Bourne Eau were made in the interests of better drainage through the low fenlands to the river Welland north of Spalding. Both rivers had been used for trade for many years, though the first formal improvement to make them navigable occurred in 1781, when the Act stated that they should be made 30 feet wide and five feet deep. These two navigations were never major commercial routes, but the traders at Bourne took advantage of the improvements and, by the beginning of the 19th century, had constructed a wharf in Eastgate. Drainage was not a problem on the river Slea nor the river Bain, and the decisions to build the Sleaford Navigation (opened in 1794) and Horncastle Navigation (opened in 1802) were taken for strictly commercial reasons. Both Acts were passed in 1792. Both navigations joined the river Witham to take advantage of the connections to the port at Boston and the river Trent. By the second half of the 18th century the river Witham's commercial importance was fully recognised, although improvements to the river Witham under the Act of 1762 were again as much to do with drainage as transport. The work was completed in just eight years, and the potential for Lincoln as an inland port was enhanced by deepening the Brayford Pool, thereby enabling navigation from the Witham to the Trent. The network of drains north of Boston was also navigable and provided local transport for both passengers and goods. But for the most part improvements to Lincolnshire's waterways did not improve the communication with the fast-developing industrial Midlands since, apart from the Fosse Dyke to river Witham connection, the schemes were isolated from each other and did not form an interlocking network. However, two canals were built which crossed the county border. The Stainforth and Keadby Canal passed through the Isle of Axholme from the river Don in South Yorkshire and joined the river Trent to provide a route to the Humber. The other purpose-built canal was between Nottingham and Grantham and was opened in 1793. Before that goods from and to the Midlands had to be barged along the river Trent to Newark and carried by packhorse and cart along the Great North Road. The Grantham Canal lost out to direct competition from the Nottingham-Grantham railway and finally closed in the 1930s, yet for the most part Lincolnshire's improved waterways survived as part of drainage schemes if not as commercial highways.

13

Railways

The transport revolution brought about by railways during the last half of the 19th century affected every aspect of life. The impact was not only on the economy of the county but also on social life and people's perceptions of progress. Unlike canals, a form of technology with which people were familiar, railways were entirely new. Few people were acquainted with steam technology, and the rapid expansion of the railway network was the technological miracle of the age. More important than the impact of the technology itself, it did much to bring to an end the county's isolation. Branch lines joined main lines and within hours passengers could be almost anywhere in the country. Lincolnshire's ports developed and the passage of goods traffic through the county for export or import increased Lincolnshire's imprtance nationally and internationally. In addition, because of the high costs of financing the railways, capital was obtained from sources beyond of Lincolnshire and therefore decisions about a particular railway's viability were often being taken by interests outside the county to an extent not seen with canals.

77 *The first railway station in Lincoln was built for the Midland Railway in 1846.*

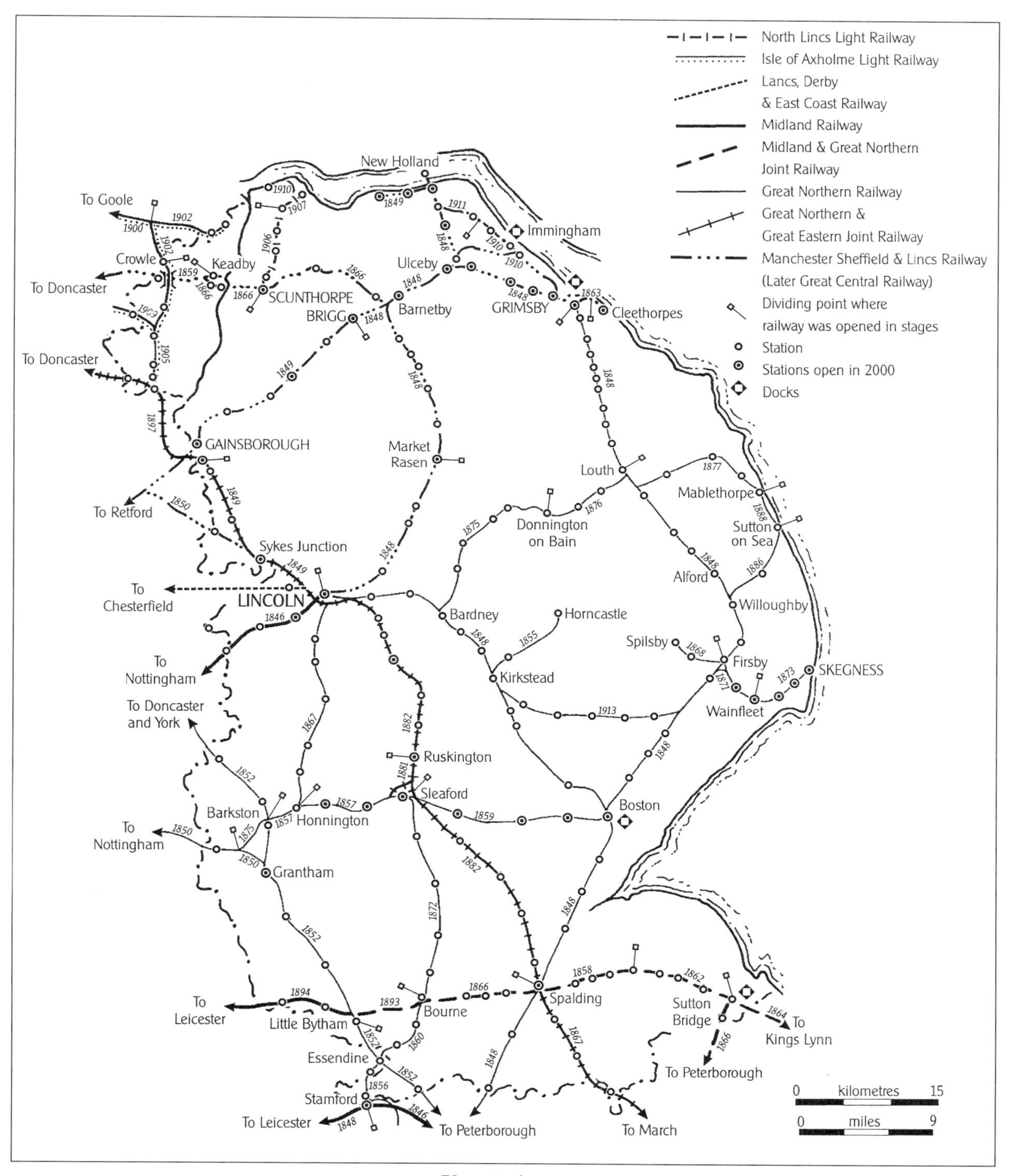
North Lincs Light Railway
Isle of Axholme Light Railway
Lancs, Derby & East Coast Railway
Midland Railway
Midland & Great Northern Joint Railway
Great Northern Railway
Great Northern & Great Eastern Joint Railway
Manchester Sheffield & Lincs Railway (Later Great Central Railway)
Dividing point where railway was opened in stages
Station
Stations open in 2000
Docks
New Holland
Immingham
To Goole
Crowle
Keadby
To Doncaster
SCUNTHORPE
BRIGG
Barnetby
Ulceby
GRIMSBY
Cleethorpes
To Doncaster
GAINSBOROUGH
Market Rasen
Louth
To Retford
Mablethorpe
Sutton on Sea
Donnington on Bain
Sykes Junction
Alford
To Chesterfield
LINCOLN
Willoughby
Bardney
Horncastle
To Nottingham
Spilsby
Firsby
Kirkstead
SKEGNESS
Wainfleet
To Doncaster and York
Ruskington
Sleaford
Barkston
Honnington
Boston
To Nottingham
Grantham
Spalding
To Leicester
Little Bytham
Bourne
Sutton Bridge
To Kings Lynn
Essendine
To Peterborough
Stamford
To Leicester
To Peterborough
To March
0 kilometres 15
0 miles 9

78 *Railways.*

There was no national railway strategy, despite the efforts of the Board of Trade, and so competing schemes by different companies were numerous. Nowhere is this better demonstrated than by the railway politics in the race from London to York to form an eastern route. Powerful interests were at work. In 1835, a committee established in Lincoln recognised the enormous potential of railways when it reported that:

> Railway transport appears destined to restore to the Eastern side of the island some of the advantages which it lost, when the discovery of America and other causes turned the current of commerce to the Western shores of Great Britain.

Nearly ten years later there were three possible trunk lines through the county. The Direct Northern Railway, via Peterborough and Gainsborough, was to pass near Lincoln at Doddington. The Eastern Counties Railway via Wisbech to Doncaster planned to take advantage of the natural Witham gap at Lincoln. The third scheme, The London & York Railway, planned to bypass almost the whole county, running through Peterborough via Grantham, Newark, and Gainsborough to Doncaster. The Direct Northern Railway was supported principally by interests from outside the county, but the Eastern Counties Railway included powerful Lincolnshire interests including Charles Chaplin of Blankney, Henry Handley of Culverthorpe, George Hussey Packe of Caythorpe and Lord Worsley. Not everyone was supportive. Colonel Charles de Laet Waldo Sibthorpe, the reactionary Tory MP for Lincoln from 1826 to 1855, whose country seat at Canwick overlooked the Witham gap at Lincoln, said about railways, 'they are public frauds and private robbers whose nefarious schemes will collapse, and the old and happy mode of travelling the turnpike roads, in chaises, carriages and stage, will be restored'.

Whilst discussions about these routes were going on, others challenged the idea of an eastern route. Most opposition came from George Hudson, the 'Railway King', whose interests lay in a Midland route to York via Leicester and Derby, and the Midland Railway supplied the first lines into the county, operating branch lines from Nottingham to Lincoln and Peterborough to Stamford which were completed in 1846 and 1848 respectively. At this time the Great Northern Railway (GNR) was advancing northwards to make a direct link to York by opening a loop line from Peterborough, via Spalding and Boston, to Lincoln. This was connected by the East Lincolnshire Railway from Boston to Louth and Grimsby and on to New Holland in 1848. There was already a ferry operating from there to Hull. The current east coast main line through Grantham, Newark and Retford was not completed until 1852 by the GNR. The south and east of the county were principally the interests of the GNR and continued to be so as smaller branch lines were developed; north Lincolnshire mostly came under the Manchester, Sheffield and Lincolnshire Railway (MSLR), which later became the Great Central Railway. By 1849 their lines connected Retford with Gainsborough, Lincoln, Market Rasen and Brigg in a large loop, and on to Grimsby and Cleethorpes, joining with the GNR line from Louth.

79 *The first M.S.L.R. train to enter Grimsby in 1848.*

80 *The construction of the Royal Dock, Grimsby,* c.*1850.*

There was an enormous impact on the towns through which these lines passed. The growth of Grimsby is a good example. In 1846 the MSLR took over the old Dock Company intending to create a new dock, although this proved less successful than was hoped. Nobody at this time could have forecast the growth of the fishing industry which was to dominate the town for over a century. From a local fishing industry before 1850, it was landing 45,000 tons of fish in 1880, a figure which had risen to 193,000 tons by 1912. Fresh fish was transported throughout the country, encouraging the growth of fish and chip shops everywhere. In 1911 the M.S.L.R. received £293,000 from this traffic alone. Boston was different, as the GNR never had a direct stake in the docks when they were improved in the early 1880s. Good communications with the rest of the country made an immediate impact and shipping use of the docks at Grimsby rose from 396 vessels in 1881 to 605 in 1894. The development in 1912 of the deep sea port of Immingham was supported by the building of an additional section of line from Grimsby, which was opened two years earlier.

Railway construction employed a large labour force of itinerant 'navvies'. The 1851 Census reveals 342 labourers out of a total population of 1,250 at Castle Bytham; 164 of 574 at Little Bytham and 184 of 958 at Corby were employed on the GNR railway between Essendine and Grantham. Their reputation preceded them. In 1845 a correspondent reported in the *Stamford Mercury* that losses were incurred through the unpaid bills of 'freeloaders', and that in some cases 'the wives of decent men and the mothers of families ... have been induced to rob their husbands and abscond'. On the other hand public houses did a roaring trade.

Iron stone was mined in Lincolnshire during the Roman period though in relatively small quantities. The transport of large quantities of ore was made possible by railways and from the 1860s Frodingham and Scunthorpe developed as a major producer of iron stone which was transported into Yorkshire to be smelted. A railway was built to take the stone from the quarries east of the Trent and the South Yorkshire Railway Company built a section in 1859 to the west bank, the two being connected by a bridge built over the river in 1866. From the beginning of the 1860s, however, iron was being produced in and around Scunthorpe, and the railways transported not the raw material but the processed iron after the Trent Iron Works opened in 1864 and the Frodingham furnace began operating a year later. By 1880 there were 21 furnaces. The good rail transport links were essential to the development of this industry and the population increased dramatically. Frodingham's rose from 113 in 1851 to 1,396 in 1901 and Scunthorpe's from 303 to 6,750 over the same period. Other lines were

81 *The Trent Iron Works.*

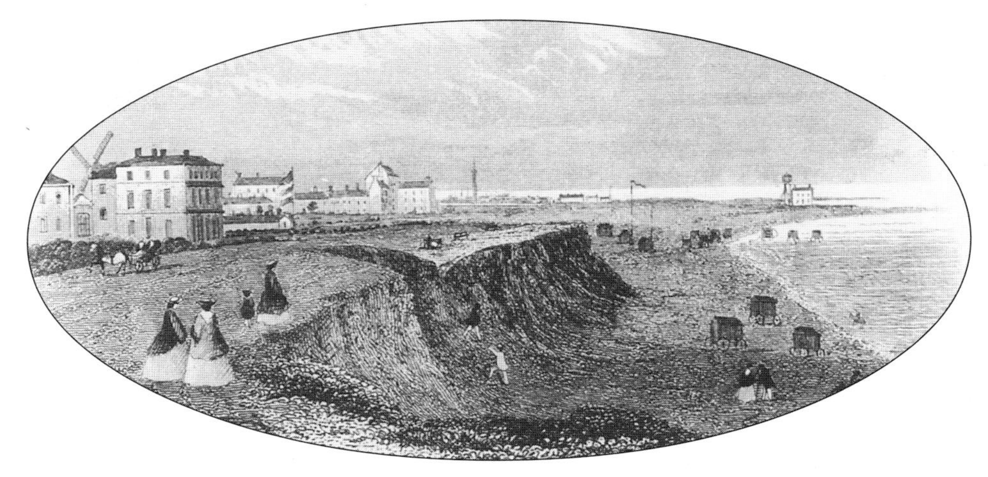

82 *The seaside at Cleethorpes with bathing machines, 1861.*

also boosted by iron-stone quarrying. Quarries were worked in a number of parishes on the Lincolnshire-Leicestershire border south of Grantham, feeding into the main London to York line. In 1867 the GNR built a line from Honington to Lincoln, which serviced a number of quarries between Leadenham and Grantham and for the first time provided Lincoln with a direct line to London.

The holiday industry developed as a direct result of the railways. At the end of the 18th century there were already some hotels and inns along the Lincolnshire coast, at Sutton in the Marsh (on Sea), Cleethorpes, Ingoldmells, Mablethorpe, Skegness, Saltfleetby, and even Fosdyke. These catered for the new fashion for sea-bathing or for people taking sea-water or taking in the fresh east-coast air for their health. At this time hotels advertised their dining rooms, smoke rooms, bars, bedrooms and hot and cold water, as well as their own bathing machines for the modesty of female bathers. However, railways enabled this small-scale activity for the relatively wealthy to change to a large-scale industry for the masses. Branch lines were constructed to Cleethorpes in 1863, Skegness in 1873, Mablethorpe in 1877 and Sutton-on-Sea in 1886 and the popularity of these resorts with workers from the industrial midland towns increased with cheap day-return tickets. Cleethorpes was promoted by the MSLR when a single-track line was extended from Grimsby in 1863. In August of that year Cleethorpes, whose population was only 1,400, attracted 30,000 visitors. The development of Skegness was even more dramatic. In 1801 Skegness' population was 134 and had risen to just 336 by the middle of the century. By the beginning of the 20th century, after connection to the railway network in 1873, it had increased to 2,140. The original line was built to Wainfleet to cater for agricultural interests, but the slump in the farming industry during the 1870s directly encouraged diversification into transport for day-trippers to Skegness. This period also coincided with the introduction of Bank Holidays, reduced working hours and, for many, an annual week's holiday. The Earl of Scarbrough planned a new town of about 700 houses on 96 acres of land

83 *Smile: from a poster advertising Mablethorpe.*

between 'Roman Bank' and the seashore. Laid out on a grid plan with wide roads converging onto a new parish church at the centre, the central avenue to the shore was originally envisaged as the main road. However, the shortest route along what is now Lumley Road, from the railway station to the sea at the south end of the development, became the commercial centre of the town. As well as promoting the building of the town, the Earl was also largely responsible for the pier, the Steamboat Company, the baths, cricket ground and the Pleasure Gardens. The impact here, too, was dramatic. Skegness (population 500) attracted 10,000 day-trippers on August Bank Holiday 1874 and by 1882 this had risen to 20,000. Numbers were such that the last train did not leave until 2 o'clock in the morning. Holiday makers were also prepared to travel from further afield. Before the railways the Lincolnshire coast was already a fashionable destination for people from as far away as London. However, once the railways arrived, they were soon catering for industrial workers from the Midlands—from Northampton, Leicester, Nottingham—from Sheffield, Rotherham and even as far away as Wigan and Manchester. John Hassall's famous painting of the Jolly Fisherman was part of an advertising campaign by GNR in 1908 to encourage 3s. (15p) return day trips, a three-hour journey from London, King's Cross.

The impact of railways on other towns *en route* may not have been so dramatic, but it was nevertheless as important. Unlike Grimsby, Boston's new dock which opened in 1884 was funded not by railway investors, but by Boston Corporation, but it could take advantage of rail links. For a short time until 1853, Boston had been the GNR's main operating base with engineering offices and workshops, until they were moved to Doncaster. Large areas of land were used for sidings, buildings, stations, engine sheds and goods yards which affected the local townscape, and large numbers of factories and warehouses were soon established alongside the lines as they had been along the canals a century earlier. Lincoln also provides a good example of the impact of railways because the routes were forced to pass through the narrow Witham gap. A large

84 *The fairground on Skegness Beach was begun in the 1870s.*

area of land in the centre of the city south of the Brayford Pool became railway sidings with various buildings, and a further, smaller area to the east of the town along the river Witham was also used. In the age of steam, coal yards for locomotives, factory power and domestic heating, were a characteristic feature of land next to all railway stations. At Sleaford the Bass Maltings were built to use the railway system. These vast six-storey buildings dominated the town and remained in operation until the 1960s. Tremendous rivalry existed between railway companies, especially when they were in direct competition. At Lincoln St Mark's station was built by the Midland Railway in 1846 but two years later a larger and altogether more impressive station was built for the GNR.

Railways did not affect water transport as greatly as in other counties. Many waterways remained in operation for many years after the arrival of railways, because they had to be maintained for drainage purposes. However, as railways were quicker and could carry greater quantities of goods than canal barges, the volume of trade through the canals and along rivers declined markedly. The prospects for water transport were not helped by the policy whereby some railway companies bought the controlling influence in canal companies. When the railway from Boston to Lincoln opened in 1848, the GNR had control of the Witham Navigation and the Fosse Dyke Canal, leasing the former for 999 years at £10,545 p.a. and the latter for 894 years at £9,570 pa. This, however, did not immediately prevent competition. Here the GNR was forced to introduce one of the few 4th class carriages in the country, priced at one halfpenny a mile, to compete with the steam packets on the river Witham between Lincoln and Boston. The speed of the train won the day, and by 1863 steam packets were out of business. The greatest impact, however, was on freight. In 1848, 278,154 tons were carried on the two waterways but by 1868 this had fallen to 85,134 tons. In 1849 the GNR was empowered by Act of Parliament to purchase the Louth Navigation. After this, the canal went into decline even though a few years later the railway company gave up its shares and control reverted to the Commissioners. The GNR had no direct shares in the Horncastle Navigation, but its impact was nevertheless as great. When the Horncastle spur opened in 1855, the dividends on the Horncastle Navigation were six per cent. The following year they were just one and a half per cent, an indication of the effect of railways on the canal system not only in Lincolnshire but throughout the country.

85 *The 'Jolly Fisherman' produced for a poster by the GNR.*

The network of village stations in the county meant that no hamlet or village was more than a dozen miles from a station, all of which were fed by carriers. Even the smallest station became the centre of commercial activity. One typical example is Spilsby station at the end of the five-mile Firsby branch from the Boston-Cleethorpes line, which had warehouses, livestock pens and coal depots as well as platforms and station buildings. Lincolnshire's main rail network was completed by 1913 when the line connecting the Boston-Lincoln with the Boston-Cleethorpes lines through Coningsby was constructed. Railways were in their heyday. Not only

86 *Post-Beeching. Part of the disused Lincoln to Honington line.*

had they affected water transport, but the coaching industry had been decimated for long-distance travel and turnpike acts were not renewed. Long-haul transport of both passengers and goods became the preserve of railways.

Railways began to change between the First and Second World Wars because of national economic decline, only to be given a boost when they became strategically important during the Second World War, not least to transport service personnel to Lincolnshire's many RAF stations. Many of these stations were served by railway stations—for example, the Royal Air Force College Cranwell made great use its own dedicated single-track line from Sleaford.

The decline in railways after nationalisation in 1947 was brought about by the increase in bus operations, car ownership, improvements to the road network and the poor state of a system deprived of investment during the war. Few were surprised when, in 1963, the Beeching Report announced that nationally 5,000 miles of railway line and some 2,000 stations were to be closed. The proposal for Lincolnshire was to close all services in the east of the county beyond Boston and Grimsby. The first line to close was the Woodhall-Boston Line but, because of opposition from local councils pleading the reliance of the east-coast tourist industry on railway communications, the line to Skegness was retained. Much of the rest of the network closed. The Honington-Lincoln line closed in 1965. The biggest year of closure was 1970, when the lines between Boston and Spalding, Lincoln to Firsby, Firsby to Grimsby and the branch from Willoughby to Mablethorpe ceased operating. Rationalisation also occurred in Lincoln with the closure of St Mark's station, after which all rail traffic was routed into Lincoln Central station—to the delight of Lincoln's motorists as one of the two railway crossings in the High Street was closed. The old Midland Railway station of St Mark's has since been incorporated into a shopping centre which bears its name, and the old sidings to the south of the Brayford Pool are the site of the new University of Lincolnshire and Humberside.

14

Rural Life between 1800 and 1850

Widespread rural violence in the form of the 'Swing Riots' erupted during the winter of 1830. It was the result of increasing tension in the country-side and was ignited by the introduction of new working practices which reduced the amount of work available during the winter months, a lean time in the farming year. The Swing Riots were named after 'Captain Swing', the fictitious hero of the rural poor who passed around the county setting fire to hay-ricks and barns and destroying the hated threshing machines. This was rural Luddism; these machines were taking away the traditional winter work of agricultural workers and, therefore, increased the threat that families might need to turn to the parish for help. This was not unique to Lincolnshire, but began in West Sussex in February 1830 and spread through the midland and eastern counties before reaching Lincolnshire, where the first instance of Swing-related arson occurred at Moulton near Holbeach, in the middle of November 1830. Tension by this time was high and anonymous letters were sent to farmers, setting out grievances and warning them of the consequences of not giving in to the writers' demands.

One such letter was clear:

> mossop you are a damd badun and you may look out we are geten gone on you with out you destroy your mysheen and get out of your farm men and sheperds and take them home to ther one [own] parish win in ten days we will burn you in all parts. weare not speaking on you a lone but all that employs them that don't belong hear so you may look out to your corn and hay. blast and buger your eyes if you do not imploy your own poor we will burn you in your bed.

INCENDIARY
FIRE.
£700.
REWARD.

WHEREAS, some Person or Persons have, THIS EVENING, maliciously SET ON FIRE A

STACK OF OATS

IN THE STACKYARD OF MR. WILLIAM [illegible], AT

BELTON, near GRANTHAM.

NOTICE IS HEREBY GIVEN,

That a Reward of £500. will be paid by the County Fire Office, for the Discovery of the Miscreant or Miscreants concerned in such Fire: to be paid on conviction of the Offender or Offenders; in addition to the Reward of £200. offered by the Committee of Magistrates, Noblemen, Gentlemen, & Others, at the Guild-hall, in Grantham, on the 8th Instant.

J. H. COLLINGWOOD, Jun.
Agent to the County Fire Office.

Little Gonerby, near Grantham,
18th December, 1830.

87 *Incendiary fire notice.*

Another letter to a farmer in Great Hale began 'Mr green as sure as you are a Bad man you may expect a visit some night before Christmas ... Mr edward dawsons men give him Bad Word so he must mind and sleep with one eye open'. It concluded, 'Bread or Blood my Boys or fire and Smoke'.

In all there were over 29 cases of arson in Lincolnshire, one of the worst tolls in the country. However, few threshing machines were destroyed, perhaps because of the quick action of landowners such as Sir Gilbert Heathcote, owner of land in Kesteven, who published a notice in *The Lincoln, Rutland and Stamford Mercury* ordering his tenant farmers to stop using them. The forces of law and order were also at work. Before the existence of a county police force, Special Constables were sworn in at 1s.

(5p) per day and 3s. (15p) per night and, in view of the developing situation, Lord Brownlow, Lord Lieutenant of the county, applied to government for 'swords and belts' to equip a horse patrol at Sleaford. By spring 1831 the Swing Riots had ended, the result of increased work on the land as winter ended, the actions of landowners and the forces of law and order.

These events illustrate the growing tension in the rural world since the end of the French wars in 1815. In 1817 the Lord Lieutenant and magistrates were evidently concerned about blasphemous and seditious pamphlets which were circulating 'in great numbers'. Nationally 1819 was a year of political tension. Meetings were held throughout the country as well as in Lincolnshire to support of a number of radical causes: extending the franchise, free trade in corn, changes to the Combination Laws and so on. Tension was such that the Kesteven magistrates, following the example of their counterparts in Lindsey, thought they should offer a Loyal Address in which they stated that these meetings were '... for the Promulgation of Mischievous and seditious doctrine and when wicked and designed Individuals with Reform in their Mouths and Revolution in their Hearts are using every artifice both by speaking and writing to mislead and poison the Public mind...'. They went on to say, 'That we will use the utmost vigilance to prevent the circulation of all blasphemous and seditious publications and to bring to Punishment the Distributors of them whenever they can be found'.

Town Hall, Grantham. ***Monday, Nov.* 29, 1830.**

The Magistrates acting for the Soke of Grantham, and the Hundreds of Winnibriggs and Threco, and Loveden, in the County of Lincoln; request that such Gentlemen and other Inhabitants as are willing to form an Association for the preservation of the public peace and protection of property, will attend at the Town Hall, in Grantham aforesaid, on **WEDNESDAY** next, the 1st of December, at Eleven o'clock in the Forenoon; to enroll themselves accordingly, and to be sworn in Special Constables if necessary.

ROBT. SCOFFIN.
W. HARDY.
JOHN TAYLOR.
J. EMINSON.
RICHD. HARVEY,
THOS. EMINSON.
Chief Constables.

STORR, PRINTER, GRANTHAM.

88 *A public notice for Special Constables.*

The traditional view of rural society is of idyllic villages of thatched cottages under the control of a paternalistic landowner where, although people were poor, they seemed content with their lot, and knew and accepted their place in the social hierarchy. This 'chocolate box' view of rural life was greatly promulgated by later Victorians in popular art and literature as a reaction against the evils—as they perceived them—of industrialisation. The reality of the rural world was different. The rural population was increasing during the first half of the 19th century to such an extent that it put a severe strain on parish and village institutions. All but a handful of Lincolnshire parishes increased in population, although the increase was not uniform throughout the county. The greatest increase took place in the large 'Open' parishes of the Fens and the coastal strip northwards to Grimsby and the parishes of the Isle of Axholme. The average population increase in the Fen parishes in the period 1800-50, excluding Boston and Spalding, was 101 per cent. This was encouraged by enclosure and the need for labour, as well as the impact of speculative builders and the lack of control by an individual dominant landowner. The 44 most 'Closed' parishes were located in the Lindsey uplands; in those with one landowner, the average increase was 55 per cent over the same

89 *The landowner.*

period—still a substantial rise. One major result of this general increase, of some concern to the authorities, was the 'growing nuisance' of vagrancy. Some saw it as a natural consequence of an 'overgrown population' but, although vagrancy was an offence, to arrest all vagrants was never a feasible solution as all the Houses of Correction would be full. Concern amongst landowners was mostly '... not their [the vagrants] disorderly conduct ... but the numbers, the danger of infection, espionage, and pernicious example to our labourers'. In 1850 an article in *The Lincolnshire, Stamford and Rutland Mercury* recognised some of the problems associated with a breakdown in traditional relationships:

> ... society loses in the disruption of all ties between the labourer and the soil in which he labours, the abrogation of all bonds of interest between him and his employer, and the removal of himself and his family from the genial influence of intercourse with the owner, and the pastor and the instructor of the village whence he has been expelled.

There certainly seems to have been a difference between those 'Closed' parishes where there were one or very few landowners and 'Open' parishes where there were many. The distinction was clear to contemporary commentators. The population in Lord Carrington's village of Humberston was described in 1813 by Arthur Young as being 'sober and industrious'. Similarly, labourers living on the estate of the Duke of Ancaster were said by Young to be remarkable for being 'orderly, decent church going men, who behaved themselves well'. In the middle of the century it was said of Lord Brownlow's recently built village of Londonthorpe that the visitor was:

> at once struck with the neatness of its newly erected, and as we supposed, model cottages and gardens, with a wash-house in common on the opposite side of the road, containing a mangle and 'other appurtenances there to belonging', not omitting to mention a useful as well as ornamental looking pump placed undercover at the entrance and for the joint use of the fortunate tenants. There has obviously been great pains bestowed upon making matters comfortable in the village. It must be solid gratification to the landowner to know that his humble cottagers are contented and grateful.

A different image is presented by Rev. Samuel Hopkinson, who described his parishioners at Morton near Bourne as follows:

> ... let the magistrates be ever so active, let the resident clergy be ever so attentive, while the property of this large parish continues divided and in so many hands, each individual proprietor will consider himself at liberty to act independently. His example is insensibly limited by his inferiors who gradually growing up in ... lawless habits, have no notion of that decent deportment and necessary subordination visible in market towns and villages belonging solely to either some virtuous nobleman, or resident gentleman.

More efficient farming, after the first impact of the labour-intensive period following enclosure and the fall in the price of corn, made farmers more economy conscious. A growing population and less work put tremendous strains on the poor-law system. Since the time of Elizabeth I, the parish was responsible for providing for its own poor through the poor rate levied on property owners. Many parishes provided their own work-house where the destitute were housed. One such example is at Bassingham,

where the parish let the workhouse at a cost of £130 per annum. To set against this cost the governor could keep the money earned by the paupers from work both inside and outside the workhouse. The governor could also keep the money obtained from the fathers of illegitimate children. Governors thus had an interest in ensuring that the inmates were as self-supporting as possible. Workhouses were meagre and overcrowded. Inventories compiled in 1830 show that at Bassingham it contained 10 bedsteads, seven beds, 14 bolsters/pillows, 13 blankets, and a number of rugs. There were also 13 chairs, six tables, a desk, a warming pan, two smoothing irons, four pans, tongs and fender, one oven and boiler, four fire grates and the obligatory bible. At Billinghay the situation was even worse. In 1830 it contained seven beds and the necessary bedding, some pots for cooking, one frying pan, four knives and forks and three spoons.

Other provisions were made. At Bassingham the parish owned 16 cottages which in 1834 were let for 1d. per month to the able-bodied poor. At Great Hale the parish rented land to the poor for 'spade husbandry' and at Morton 22 tenements were let. Parishes also provided a dole. For example, extracts from the first page of the Navenby Vestry Book state:

> Widow Woolfitt, Widow More, Robert Simpson, Jane Chapman's child 1s. 6d. per week each ...
>
> That the following allowance to be paid to Elizabeth Bailey's bastard child 1s. 6d. ...

Such provision was not uncommon. Boston had had a workhouse in 1730, Bourne in 1735 and the parish of St Swithin in Lincoln in 1737. Those parishes that could not support their own workhouse had to rely entirely on outdoor relief. By the beginning of the 19th century perhaps only 20 per cent of Lincolnshire parishes had their own, although between 60 and 70 parishes had combined together for greater efficiency based at Winterton, Caistor, Wainfleet All Saints, Claypole and Lincoln.

90 *The labourer.*

It is difficult to calculate how many people were in receipt of relief. Figures for Billinghay in the early 1830s suggest that approximately 20 per cent of families were being relieved in one form or another. If the average figure for the whole county was actually between 10 and 20 per cent, then a large number of the total population was reliant on the parish for poor relief. The highest proportion of parish rate was spent on the poor. For example, at Billinghay one year's expenditure on the poor came to £448, compared with £39 spent on the Highways and £81 on the Constable. One problem was finding work for the poor to do. Frequently, they were put to work on the highways for which the parish had responsibility. Some parishes adopted a Balloting System, whereby farmers were allocated labourers in proportion to the rateable value of their land. For example, at the Vestry meeting at Bassingham at the end of December 1829, 15 labourers were listed in need of work. A division of 15 into the total rate meant that each labourer was equal to approximately £80 of rateable value. Farmers were grouped to achieve a sum divisible by £80

91 *Haymaking.*

and labourers were allocated on that basis. Therefore, Mr. Brocklebank, the largest landowner in Bassingham with land rated at £224, and Mr. Burt with £27, combined came to £251 and were entitled to three labourers between them.

The lower population in 'Closed' parishes and tighter control by the dominant owners meant that the problem of excess labour was less acute. Landowners were less likely to allow new housing and, indeed, some owners demolished houses to prevent unwanted labourers moving into 'their' parish. For example, Thomas Rawnsley, the Vice Chairman of the Spilsby Poor Law Union, reported, '... with one or two exceptions it has been the practice of pulling down cottages, or not building them, which has been occurring for nearly thirty years'. This was done to prevent the poor becoming a burden on the Poor Rate although Rawnsley stated that this was 'not the only reason but the one that outweighs the others'. This method of control was adopted in some 'Closed' parishes but many landowners also had a paternalistic attitude to their labourers. The provision of schools was common and charity was also important. Charitable giving in 'Open' parishes was often the result of ancient bequests and was administered by the Vestry, in 'Closed' parishes it was often done from a sense of paternalistic duty on the part of the landowner. For example, in 1830 Sir Gilbert Heathcote responded to the problem of unemployment in Folkingham—and other parishes where he had an interest—by providing food. This may also have been prompted by an increased level of discontent amongst the labouring poor, but correspondence with his agent Thomas Syson suggests that he was concerned for the welfare of his tenants and that this provision was an annual act of charity. He ordered that £25 be given to the poor at Oakham, Uppingham and Empingham to be 'disposed of in the same way as last year'. He went on to say:

> Now what should I do about Lincolnshire—let me know by return Post what you [Syson] think about it ... I am told there is general distress at Grantham, and as I am a proprietor in that Parish, would a donation there do good ...

A week later (26 December 1830) he had apparently changed his mind about Grantham stating, 'Better not be sending anything to Grantham as I am no great proprietor there'. However, he wrote a further letter to Syson '... that no time may be lost in ordering the distribution of Butchers Meat to the poor of Lincolnshire ...'. Charitable giving by Willoughby de Eresby, whose seat was at Grimsthorpe, was at a similar level. On Christmas Day 1831 he had distributed £96 5s. worth of meat to 132 individuals. A month later he gave wood to 27 local poor of whom 11 were widows. The Dame Margaret Thorold's Charity also provided for the distribution of wheat and flour to the poorest in Sedgbrook, Syston, Marston, Quarrington and Rauceby.

Throughout the period after the French Wars the cost of keeping the poor, which was falling on parishes, was rising. Vestries, particularly in 'Open' parishes, began to make use of the Laws of Settlement in an

attempt to control their expenditure by removing unwanted labourers and their families. These laws made it possible for each parish to determine whether an individual was its responsibility or that of another parish. Legal settlement could be gained in a number of ways: first by serving as a parish officer, second by paying parish rates, third by becoming bound as an apprentice, and fourth by being employed for one year in the parish. The basis of the system was that Settlement Certificates issued by a parish provided proof of settlement in the home parish if an individual and his family wanted to live elsewhere. The certificate was often insisted on by the receiving parish as an insurance against the family becoming chargeable on the poor rate should they become unemployed. Parishes were prepared to support only their own poor. If a person did not have

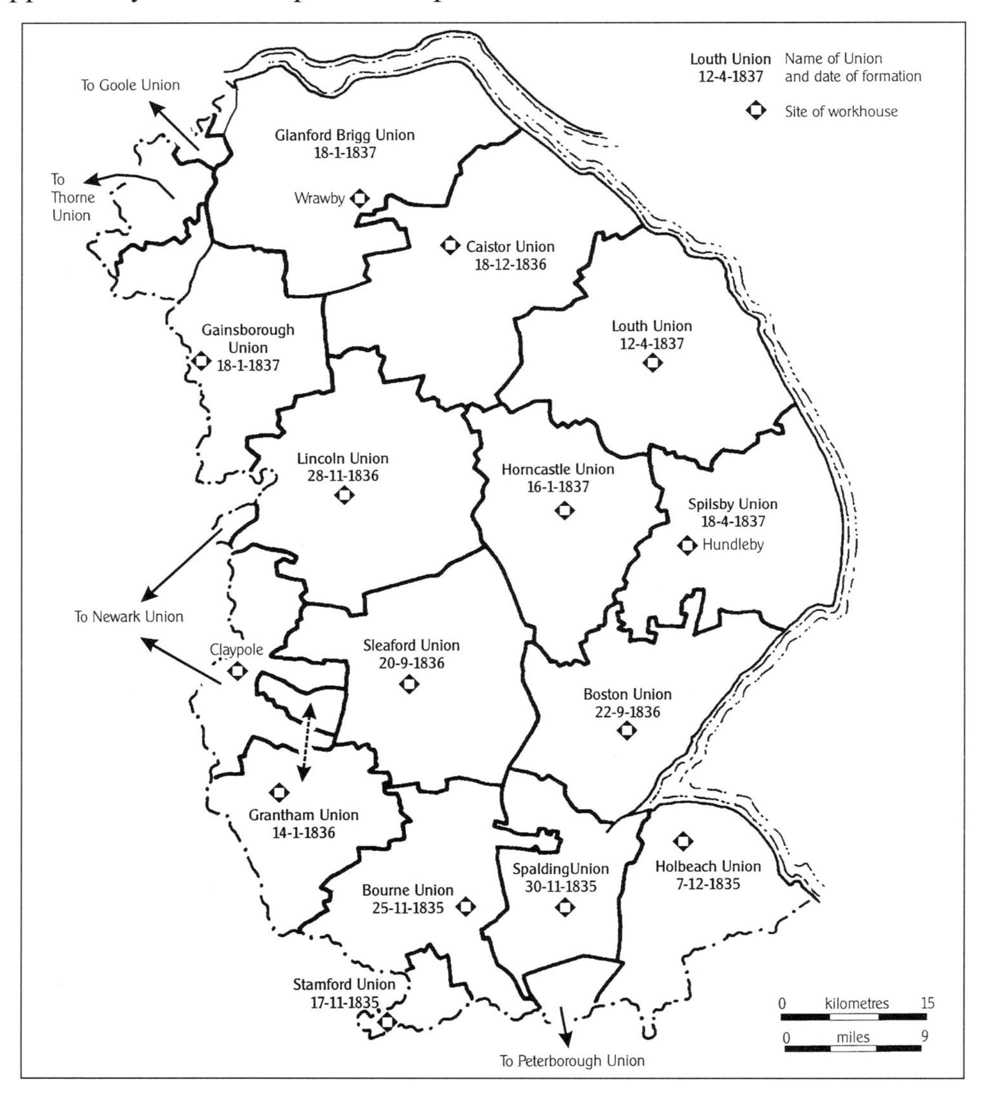

92 *The structure of the Lincolnshire Poor Law after 1834.*

a Settlement Certificate and, therefore, had no legal right of settlement and was likely to become a financial burden on the new parish, the case was examined by a magistrate to ascertain legal right of settlement. This process could lead to protracted disagreement between parishes and involved them in an unprecedented level of bureaucracy. Between 1800 and 1850, 20 of the most 'Open' parishes in Kesteven removed 569 individuals while eight of the most 'Closed' parishes removed only 33 people. Of the Open parishes the Vestry at Bourne was the most active and 110 people were removed; at Deeping St James 84, and at Sleaford 55. The table below refers to the 28 sample parishes and is indicative of the use of the Settlement Laws during the first half of the 19th century.

Years	Number of Removal Certificates	Years	Number of Removal Certificates
1800-04	8	1825-29	152
1805-09	15	1830-34	146
1810-14	29	1835-39	21
1815-19	120	1840-44	8
1820-24	104	1845-49	0

These figures include entire families which could be an expensive burden; the loss of a job by the breadwinner brought the whole family onto the poor rate. For example, Thomas Maplebeck became unemployed in Billinghay in 1828 and he himself, his wife Elizabeth, and their children Jackson (12), Thomas (10), David (8), William (6), Wheatly (4), Samuel (2), and Elizabeth (6 months) were removed to North Kyme. Pregnant spinsters also could prove expensive since the expense of confinement, care and relief had to be borne by the parish. The cost to the parish of Ruskington, in the case of Thedoria Houslan, between December 1831 and October 1832 was £10 3s. 4d. This included the cost of apprehending Wad Thurlby of Kalby, the reputed father.

The increase in the poor law costs and the associated rise in poor rates meant that the whole poor law system had to be overhauled. In 1834 the government introduced the Poor Law Amendment Act, which forced parishes to combine to form Poor Law Unions, thus removing the power of parishes to control their own affairs. This removal from the parish to an extra parochial body was the first major change in the parish's control of its own affairs, a process which was to continue throughout the century. Parishes were forced to dispose of their own workhouses and to send their poor to new institutions—utilitarian, stark, red-brick buildings where husbands were separated from their wives and children and where conditions were no better than could be found outside. Lincolnshire was quick to respond to this new development. By the middle of 1837 the county was divided into 14 Unions. Workhouses were located at Caistor, Louth, Lincoln, Horncastle, Sleaford, Boston, Grantham, Bourne, Spalding and Holbeach. The Spilsby Union workhouse was in the neighbouring parish of Hundleby and the Newark Union workhouse

was at Claypole. The Gainsborough Union also included Nottinghamshire parishes, the Grantham Union some Leicestershire parishes and the Stamford Union only a few Lincolnshire parishes, but parishes from Northamptonshire, Huntingdonshire and Rutland. A few parishes in the Isle of Axholme were included in the Thorne and Goole Unions, and Crowland went to Peterborough.

Rural populations declined in the second half of the 19th century. The Fen parishes, where the population had risen dramatically during the previous 50 years, declined by 11 per cent and the single-owner parishes had an almost static average population. Farmers adopted new machinery and methods during the agricultural boom of the mid-Victorian period, and this began to reduce the need for labour which was made worse by the depression of the last quarter of the century. During this period labourers began to migrate in larger numbers from the country-side to the new industrial centres.

The Parts of Kesteven, In the County of Lincoln. *To the Churchwardens and Overseers of the Poor of the* Parish *of* Billinghay *in the said Parts, and to the Churchwardens and Overseers of the Poor of the* Parish of Digby *in the* said Parts *and to each and every of them.*

UPON the Complaint of the Churchwardens and Overseers of the Poor of the Parish of Billinghay in the said Parts of Kesteven, unto us whose Names are hereunto set and Seals affixed, being Two of His Majesty's Justices of the Peace in and for the said Parts of Kesteven, and one of us of the Quorum, that Peter Harrod and Elizabeth his Wife and their six children John aged seventeen years Phebe aged thirteen years, Henry aged eleven years, Peter aged five years, and Elizabeth aged three years did lately come to inhabit in the said Parish of Billinghay not having gained a legal Settlement there, nor producing any Certificate owning them to be settled elsewhere, and that the said Peter Harrod and Elizabeth his Wife and their children John, Phebe, Maria, Henry, Peter, and Elizabeth are actually become chargeable to the said Parish of Billinghay We the said Justices, upon due Proof made thereof, as well upon the Examination of the said Peter Harrod upon Oath, as otherwise, and likewise upon due Consideration had of the Premises, do adjudge the same to be true; AND WE do likewise adjudge that the lawful Settlement of them the said Peter Harrod and Elizabeth his Wife and their said six children John, Phebe, Maria, Henry, Peter, and Elizabeth is in the said Parish of Digby in the said Parts of Kesteven. We do therefore require you the said Churchwardens and Overseers of the Poor of the said Parish of Billinghay or some or one of you, to convey the said Peter Harrod and Elizabeth his Wife and their said six children John, Phebe, Maria, Henry, Peter, and Elizabeth from and out of your said Parish of Billinghay, to the said Parish of Digby and them to deliver to the Churchwardens and Overseers of the Poor there, or to some or one of them, together with this our Order, or a true Copy thereof: AND WE do also hereby require you the said Churchwardens and Overseers of the Poor of the said Parish of Digby to receive and provide for them as Inhabitants of your Parish.

GIVEN under our Hands and Seals the 4th Day of February in the Year of our Lord One Thousand Eight Hundred and Thirty-Three.

93 *An order to remove a family of eight from Billinghay to Digby.*

15

19th-Century Industry and the Growth of Towns

At the beginning of the 19th century the relationship between market towns and countryside tended to be blurred. For the most part, the county's towns functioned as social centres for the local gentry, as providers of rural trades and centres of agricultural services. Regional towns such as Alford (population in 1801: 1,040), Bourne (1,664) Caistor (1,022), Horncastle (2,017), Sleaford (1,596), Spalding (3,296), and Louth (4,258) continued their traditional function as market towns, holding weekly markets and providing a range of rural trades and services. Country lawyers, doctors, auctioneers, bakers, blacksmiths, boot and shoe makers, bricklayers, butchers and cattle dealers, coal and corn merchants, coopers, millers, brewers and maltsters, wheelwrights, ropemakers, tailors, plumbers and painters were all to be found in these towns. All of them, except Alford, had a canal or navigable river connection by the early part of the century, making them important distribution points for coal and other goods and collection centres for grain. The canal joining Louth with the Humber estuary provided an important link high onto the Wolds, and Sleaford became the furthest point inland to be served by a canal. For the most part, canals brought about the consolidation or expansion of existing trades rather than new ones. By the beginning of the 19th century both Louth and Sleaford contained a thriving commercial centre of wharves, warehouses and yards.

Lincoln, the largest town in the county with a population of 7,193 in 1801, had not developed far beyond Daniel Defoe's 1724 description of it as '... an ancient, ragged, and still decaying city ...'. Despite this, Lincoln was at the centre of Georgian high county society and the area 'up-hill' was the centre of 'county' life. The richest and most fashionable families spent the season in London, but Lincoln society consisted of clergy, lawyers, doctors and members of the gentry. The calendar was punctuated with official and social functions, assizes, quarter sessions, visitations and races. The Assembly Rooms were built in 1744, and annual charity balls were held there attended by the county's worthies. Race week also offered social opportunities, and the racecourse moved from Canwick to Welton and then to Carholme at the beginning of the 19th century. These were glittering occasions. New theatres were built, the first in 1744 on Castle Hill. Lincoln also boasted three newspapers by 1800, a sure sign of its status as a regional capital: *The Lincoln*

94 *Lincoln in 1743.*

Gazette established in 1728, followed by *The Lincoln Journal* in 1744 and, most important of all, *The Lincoln, Rutland and Stamford Mercury*, which began publication at Lincoln in 1784. In contrast, Stamford met with Defoe's approval and he described it as 'a very fair, well built, considerable and wealthy town'. No doubt his opinion was influenced by stately Burghley House, which added to the genteel air of respectability. Stamford too, far enough from Lincoln, developed its own social life, attracting the rural élite from Leicestershire, Rutland and Northamptonshire. Assembly Rooms were built there in 1717 and plays were performed at the Guildhall until a new theatre was built in 1768. As at Lincoln, race week was the most important event on the social calendar, particularly after the event was found a permanent home south of the town in 1766 and a grandstand was erected. Fox hunting, bowls, cock-fighting, cards and bull running were all occasions which catered for the varying interests of the local and surrounding population and the social needs of the local people of all classes. At the end of the 18th century Stamford had the overall appearance of a bustling town, helped by the Great North Road, and it was much busier than Lincoln. It boasted some excellent hotels and inns including the *George*, which Defoe described as 'one of the greatest Inns in England'.

During the first half of the 19th century there was an unprecedented increase in the county's population from 208,624 in 1801 to 407,222 in 1851. This increase was not evenly spread throughout the county, because the towns began to reflect the growing importance of industries other than agriculture. A general increase in population of the countryside during the first half of the 19th century was eclipsed by the even more rapid increase in most Lincolnshire towns. In the 18th century their function as regional market centres had been closely tied to agriculture, as they had been in the Middle Ages. However, by 1850, because of new industrial development and house building, they had become distinct and separate from their rural surroundings. During the second half of the century population growth in Lincolnshire towns contrasted sharply with rural areas, where 79 per cent of rural parishes had declining populations during this period. Much of the new labour-saving farm machinery was being manufactured in the larger towns, in some cases on a substantial scale. The table below shows the population of the principal towns in Lincolnshire in 1801, 1851 and 1901, and the percentage increase between 1801-51 and 1851-1901. Those places that had become involved in large-scale commercialisation—Gainsborough, Grantham, Lincoln and Grimsby—show an enormous population increase throughout the century, compared with those that did not.

	1801	1851	per cent increase	1901	per cent increase/decrease
Alford	1040	2262	117	2478	9
Boston	5926	15132	155	16174	7
Bourne	1664	3717	123	4361	20
Caistor	1022	2407	135	1767	-26
Gainsborough	4506	7261	61	17740	144
Grantham	4288	10870	153	16467	51
Great Grimsby	1524	8860	479	36857	316
Horncastle	2015	5017	149	4118	-18
Lincoln	7193	17533	143	48268	175
Louth	4258	10553	147	9619	-9
Sleaford	1596	3539	122	3934	11
Spalding	3296	8829	167	9381	6
Stamford	4022	7332	82	7218	-2

The population of Louth increased by 147 per cent during the first half of the century, Spalding by 167 per cent, Sleaford by 121 per cent and Stamford by 82 per cent, but during the second half of the century their populations changed little. Other market towns, such as Horncastle and Caistor, were similar. The number of houses required for this increased population was enormous. Brick-making became a major industry throughout the county, providing red brick for the rows of terraced houses which are common in all Lincolnshire towns and villages. Most large towns, and many villages, had their own brickworks. In the mid-1820s there were only 35 brick and tile works but demand was such

X *Marshall's of Gainsborough and 19th-century housing between the River Trent and the railway.*

XI *Market Deeping has expanded substantially.*

XII *Grimsby Docks.*

XIII *The Humber Bridge.*

that this rose to a peak of 187 by the 1880s. The new towns made other advances. Sleaford's streets were paved and drained between 1829 and 1831, lit by gas lights from 1839 and a new Town Hall or Sessions House, described in 1856 as a 'spacious and elegant building', was built during the same period. At Louth a gasworks was opened in 1826, a year after an Act of Parliament was obtained, 'for paving, lighting, cleansing, regulating, and otherwise improving ... Louth'. The prosperity of Spalding at this time is indicated by the rebuilding of 'most of its public buildings' during 1825-56, although the General Improvement Act was not obtained until 1853, allowing for a Corn Exchange which was erected by 1856. The construction of corn exchanges stamped the importance of these market towns on their surroundings. Louth's had been erected in the 'Italian Style' in 1853 and Sleaford's was opened in 1857.

The entry in White's 1856 *Directory* for Louth shows a town with craftsmen and traders tied to the rural economy: auctioneers, blacksmiths, cattle and horse dealers, corn merchants, corn millers, maltsters, machine makers, wheelwrights, cowkeepers, curriers and leather manufacturers. A similar pattern was to be found in most other market towns in Lincolnshire at this time. Even Boston, once the pre-eminent port of the country, stagnated during the second half of the 19th century after a period of tremendous population growth, as trade became increasingly concentrated on the west-coast port of Liverpool or London and the south coast ports. Boston's geographical position was probably the main reason for the initial success and later failure of engineering there. William Howden built at Boston in 1827 the first steam engine to be made in Lincolnshire. William Webb Tuxford became the dominant engineering enterprise in the town when he established the 'Boston and Skirbeck Iron Works', building a wide range of agricultural

95 *Typical early 19th-century labourers' brick cottages at Horncastle.*

96 *The magnificent Louth Corn Exchange built in 1853.*

machinery including threshing machines and the important portable steam engines, which were successfully exported to Scandinavia, eastern Europe and as far away as Australia. However, Boston's position, remote from raw materials of iron, steel and coal, was to become more of a problem particularly during the agricultural depression of the last quarter of the century. Tuxford was forced to close in the 1880s. Although the port had passed its heyday, Boston's position in the Fens allowed it to retain a level of commercial activity; the new dock was opened in 1884 and the channel to the Wash improved to allow the passage of sea-going vessels.

Only four Lincolnshire towns substantially increased their populations during the second half of the century. Grimsby's growth of 316 per cent was due to enormous railway investment in the new dock and its concentration on deep-sea fishing. If the increase of neighbouring Clee with Weelsby is also taken into account, the population rose from 5,122 in 1801 to 75,835 a century later. On the western side of the county, however, there was real industrial growth. Here, Gainsborough, Grantham and Lincoln established agricultural engineering enterprises, which were to become dominant throughout the country during the boom in British farming between 1850 and 1875, and they exported their products throughout the world. Gainsborough traditionally owed its prosperity to its position on the river Trent. This prosperity increased after the town became a port in its own right in 1841, when goods no longer had to receive clearance from the Hull customs. A number of mills were in operation during the first half of the century, crushing seeds imported from Europe and the Middle East to produce light oils for the engineering industry. At the same time, Smith's of Gainsborough were building vessels of up to 800 tons. These undertakings required a substantial financial investment with a relatively large labour force, although it is debatable whether they could be called factories as they did not employ the mass-production techniques or extra-human power of water or steam characteristic of factories associated with the industrial revolution.

The change in Gainsborough's status as a port did not bring about the expected growth; instead it was the beginning of a gradual decline which continued for the rest of the century. The building of railways gave a temporary boom to the port through the transport of raw materials, but it also had a detrimental effect. Gainsborough was described in 1882 as 'among those river ports which have been much injured by the railways'. Railways had a disastrous effect on the port, but helped to encourage other facets of the local economy. Marshall's Engineering, which opened in 1848, was to become a major employer. The building of the railway through Gainsborough in 1849 encouraged Marshall's to move to a 28-acre rail-side site in 1856, where raw materials could be imported from the Sheffield foundries and where they built portable steam engines for powering agricultural machinery, for export to every part of the country. By the turn of the century Marshall's was by far the biggest employer with 3,600 workers and Gainsborough had become a typical

company town. Whilst Marshall's produced general steam engines, the most successful engineering companies concentrated on the mechanisation of the agricultural industry, which took off during the second half of the century. Both Grantham and Lincoln developed such industries which gained international reputations by the end of the century. At Grantham, the firm of Richard Hornsby dominated the town, where he had successfully developed his movable steam engine and won first prize, against stiff competition, for his 8hp engine at the Great Exhibition in 1851. He also won first prize at the Universal Agricultural Exposition at Paris in 1856 as well as first prizes at numerous county shows throughout England. Engineering of this kind was still a new industry and most other firms of this type started from small beginnings. Establishing a smithy to manufacture and repair farming implements at Spittlegate in 1810—a fortunate location as the railway was later to run nearby—by 1854 his works were operating 34 furnaces. His principal products were steam-powered threshing machines and also a seed drill, oil cake bruiser, and a successful self-binding harvester. By the end of the century Hornsby's had diversified, producing machinery for the South African gold mining industry, electric generators and, after 1891, the oil-powered internal combustion engine. By 1905 Hornsby's were employing 2,000 workmen, and thus were supporting about a third of the entire population of Grantham. The Spittlegate area of Grantham had been transformed by rows of workmen's houses and factory buildings. Its population had risen from under 500 in 1801 to over 6,500 a hundred years later. The largest growth of 226 per cent was during the 40 years after 1841. Other engineering companies also thrived: in 1877 the Phoenix Iron Works was

97 *Hornsby's seed drill, 1851.*

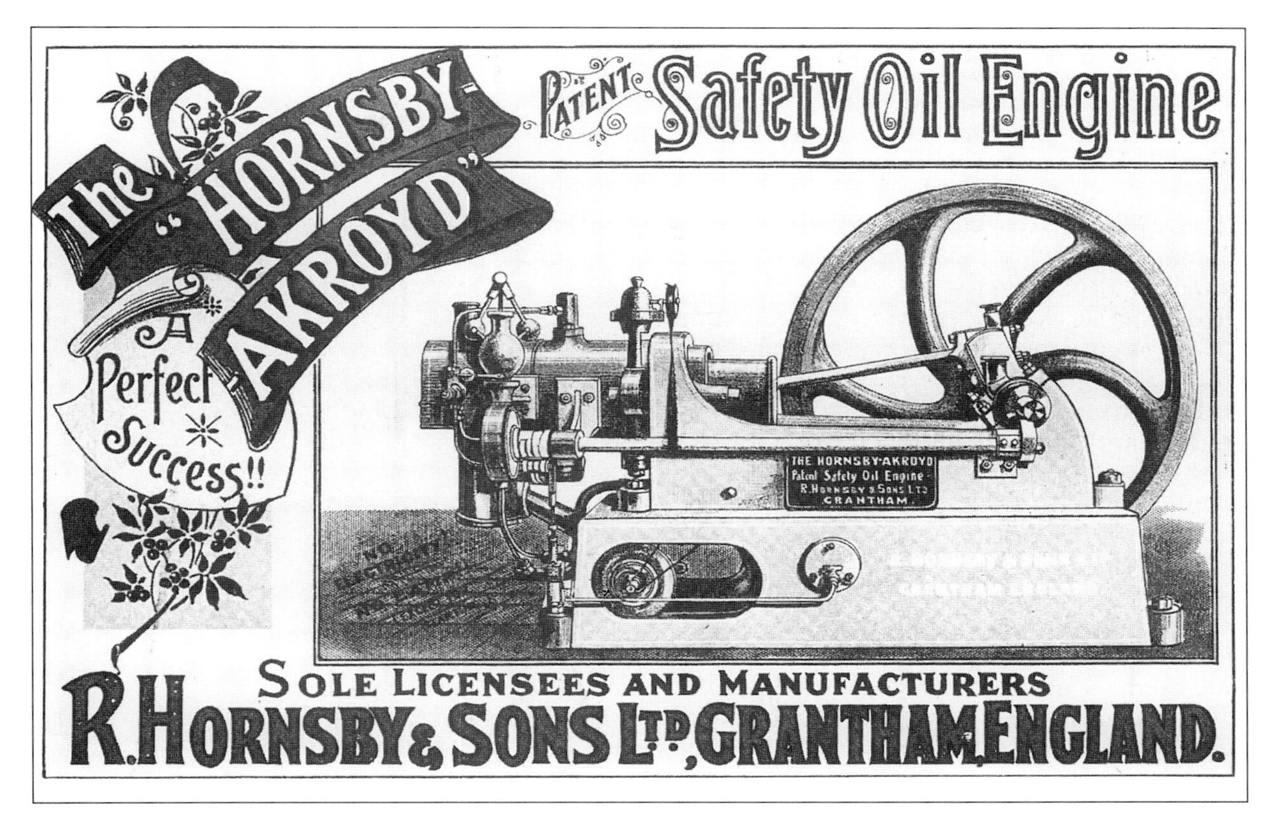

98 *The 'Hornsby Akroyd' safety oil engine, 1892.*

established by the Hampstead family to produce agricultural implements and steam engines.

Engineering was important in Gainsborough and Grantham but its impact on the economy and growth of Lincoln was even more profound. As at Gainsborough and Grantham, engineering developed during the second half of the 19th century. White's 1856 *Directory* lists the numerous merchants, trades and professions necessary to provide for a city of 17,000 people, the largest town in the county at that time. It also lists six 'iron-founders and engineers', which included Clayton Shuttleworth & Co., already located at their Stamp End Iron Works; Robey and Scott on Canwick Road; and Proctor and Burton, who a year later would join with Joseph Ruston and occupied premises on Waterside. William Foster began his engineering business in 1851, though in 1856 White still lists him under his original occupation as merchant and miller. He soon began making steam engines and threshing machines and had a workforce of 44 in 1861. This number increased to 200 by 1885. Robert Robey established his factory in 1854 and by 1864 had a workforce of 114 producing portable steam engines and threshing machines; he later added traction engines and steam ploughs, which were exported as far as Australia and South America. Nathaniel Clayton and Joseph Shuttleworth went into partnership in 1842. Clayton had established a foundry at Stamp End

and Shuttleworth a boat-building business next door. They began producing pipes and bridges, and undertook railway work; their first large-scale contract was for pipes for the Boston Water Works. By 1848 they were building steam engines and threshing machines and employed around 100 hands. They successfully exhibited at the 1851 Great Exhibition and three years later the numbers employed had risen six fold. Their first catalogue was produced in 1850 and was translated into German and French for the Paris Exhibition of 1855. The marketing potential of Europe was soon realised and Clayton and Shuttleworth steam engines were soon operating in Austria, Hungary and Turkey and the company had opened branches in Vienna, Prague and Cracow. In addition their engines were supplied to Canada, Australia, Egypt and South America. By 1870 they had a work-force of 1,200 and made 1,000 engines and 900 threshing machines a year. Clayton and Shuttleworth was large not only by national but also by international standards, equalling the size of Krupp in Germany. In 1849 John Burton and James Toyne Proctor went into partnership as millwrights and general smiths, producing agricultural implements and machines. They were soon joined by Joseph Ruston. Burton left in 1859 and Proctor sold out to Ruston in 1865. At the end of the decade Ruston was building locomotives for the Great Eastern Railway, steam excavators, road rollers and tractors and at the end of the century had expanded to occupy a 52-acre site.

The impact of them and others, such as Richard Duckering and Clarke's Crank and Forge Company, on the growth of the city was considerable. The concentration of engineering firms in the river Witham valley was constrained by susceptibility to flooding. Thus the city expanded eastward, north of the river Witham, and westward north of the Brayford

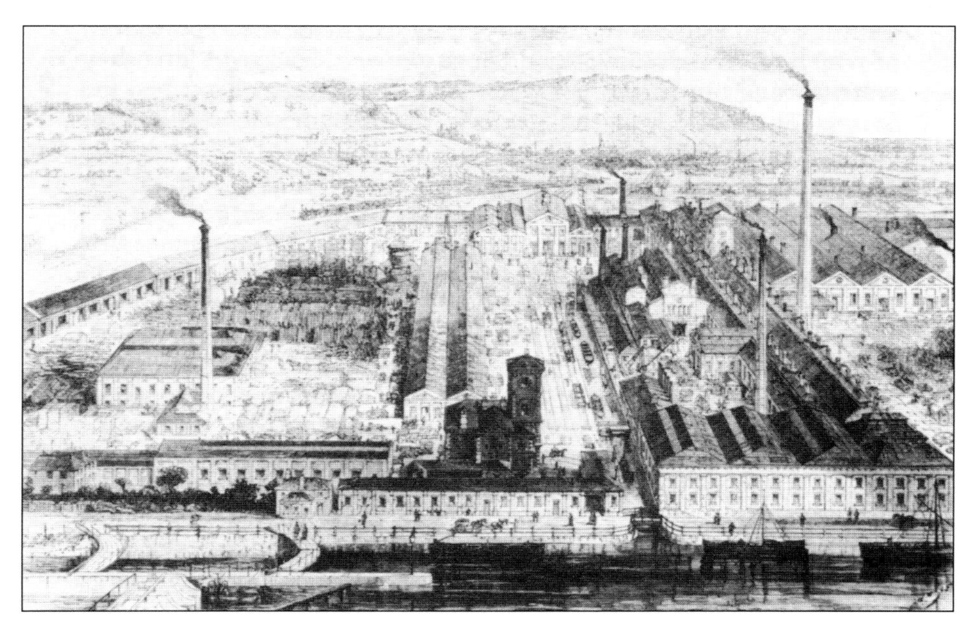

99 *The Clayton and Shuttleworth Stamp End Works, Lincoln, 1869.*

100 *The Clayton and Shuttleworth combined threshing and dressing machine, 1851.*

Pool. However, most growth occurred southward into Wigford. The population of the parishes of St Mary-le-Wigford increased by 401 per cent, St Peter-at-Gowts, 529 per cent, and St Botolph, 497 per cent between 1851 and 1901. By the end of the century this industrial centre was distinguishable by rows of terraced red-brick houses and by tall chimneys bellowing black smoke from steam engines and furnaces.

Whilst the industrial towns were experiencing sustained growth during the whole of the 19th century, market towns were undergoing limited growth or even decline. They remained the centres of agricultural activity. Bourne's population increased by 20 per cent, Sleaford's by 11 per cent and Alford, Spalding and Boston by less than 10 per cent during the second half of the century, and Stamford, Louth, Horncastle and Caistor declined. When Stamford lost out to Peterborough for the route of the main east-coast railway line the town's fate was sealed. It failed to develop a strong industrial base and even hotel and boarding services provided for the traveller were not needed as railways became the cheap and fast method of travel. However, perhaps because of Stamford's connection with road transport, Hayes & Son built a substantial factory producing coaches and carts from the 1820s but it was in decline by 1900 and finally closed in 1924. A number of Lincolnshire market towns had foundries supplying local agricultural needs. However, these were small-scale trades and few were to develop beyond this. At Louth, for example, small-scale engineering works in the name of Aswell's Iron Works, the Newmarket Iron Works and Joseph Morton's iron foundry were producing a wide range of domestic and agricultural implements during the second half of the 19th century. At Sleaford, William Henry Smith and Co. manufactured steam ploughs and John Henry Payne operated a brass and iron foundry. Despite the diversification of commercial activity during the 19th century, agriculture remained at its foundation.

16

Religious Diversity

While 19th-century Lincolnshire folk were experiencing enormous changes in their economic lives there were equally important changes occurring in their spiritual lives. These changes reflected national developments but Lincolnshire's agricultural background influenced the county's response. Religious belief became fragmented and polarised. The Anglican Church, which was not only at the physical centre of the village but since the Reformation had been the centre of traditional religious adherence, began to lose its influence over a large proportion of the rural population as the appeal of 'popular' Protestantism and Nonconformity began to claim a share of the congregation. Methodism was to capture very large congregations by the middle of the century. At the other end of the religious spectrum, the influence of Roman Catholicism increased, particularly after the 1829 Catholic Emancipation Act and the subsequent re-establishment of the Catholic hierarchy of bishops to England for the first time since the Reformation. However, Catholicism never regained much of a foothold in Lincolnshire. According to the 1851 Census of Religious Worship, Catholics were confined to pockets of activity at places such as Stamford, which attracted 7.5 per cent of the total worshippers on census day. The figure was even lower in Bourne, Caistor, Grimsby and Market Rasen. More important than the number attending Catholic churches was the impact of Catholicism on a section of the Church of

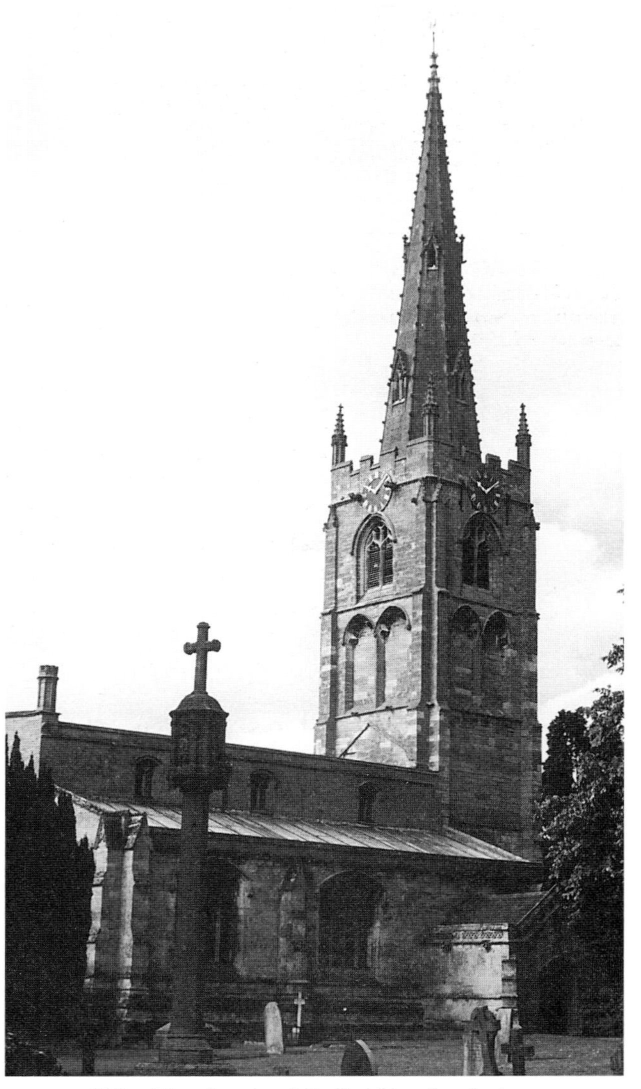

101 *The church of St Swithin, Leadenham.*

England. The High Church/neo-Catholic wing of the Anglican tradition obtained a new momentum during the first half of the 19th century after finding a voice in the Oxford Movement and a renewed interest nationally in medievalism. In Lincolnshire, however, this impact was relatively limited.

The Bishop of Lincoln, Bishop Kaye, was certainly not of this persuasion but nevertheless had to deal with one of his priests who challenged his doctrinal lead. At Leadenham, at the end of the 1830s and at the beginning of the following decade, events unfolded which resulted in conflict between the traditional dominant Anglican landowner, Col. Reeve, and the rector, Bernard Smith. The disagreement developed over the introduction, by Smith, of Popish ceremony into the parish church. Reeve's specific complaint related to the 'gaudy' decorations in the chancel, the use of Latin, the introduction of elaborate candlesticks on the front of the communion table, the practice of bowing to the altar, teaching the children to do likewise and teaching the assumption of the Blessed Virgin Mary. Bishop Kaye was drawn into the affair and there was a visitation of Leadenham at the beginning of 1841. This was reported in December in *The Stamford and Rutland Mercury* as follows:

> The zeal of the Bishop of Lincoln against the coming revival of Popish mummeries of the Church of England, has lately been put to the test by the young rector of Leadenham, who, it seems, is a disciple of the crew who are seeking to acquire a despotism over the human mind like that wielded by the parent-church through the means of her pomp and ceremony, and the engendering of superstition. In the fervency of his desire to revive the decaying influence of the priesthood, his enthusiastic reverence, it seems introduced to the church a movable cross, and an altar with a pair of candlesticks and burning tapers, the administering of the holy eucharist at an early hour in the morning by taper-light ... on the roof of the building the litany is painted in Latin.

Clearly neither the Bishop nor the writer of the report was in favour of these changes since the article concluded:

> These things and various devices and ceremonies calculated to impress the ignorant mind with awe for the mysteries of religion and its priesthood, the Bishop, we are informed, has ordered to be removed and the plain decorum of the church-service to be observed, in lieu of the pomp and show approximating to that of the Roman Catholic chapel.

In December 1842 Bernard Smith left Leadenham and, in due course, converted to Catholicism. Throughout most of the 19th century Lincoln Cathedral had a reputation for being 'low' church until, and perhaps surprisingly, the 'high' churchman Edward King was enthroned as Bishop in 1885. He caused consternation not only in Lincolnshire by wearing a mitre and other vestments, thereby laying himself open to the charge of promoting 'Priestcraft'.

The attack on Smith was not so difficult to understand as many Lincolnshire parishes at the beginning of the century were controlled by an extremely close alliance of the established church and landed interests. In some parishes there was an obvious link: at Temple Bruer, Charles Chaplin; at Ashby, Clifford King; at Newton (by Folkingham), Sir William Welby and at Aswarby, Sir Thomas Whichcote were the dominant

landowners, and Rev. Henry Chaplin, Rev. Edward Thorold, Rev. John King and Rev. Richard Whichcote were the respective incumbents. There were also numerous examples throughout the county of clergy being substantial landowners in their own right. Even if the relationship between landed interests and the Anglican church was not so obvious, the physical closeness was there for all to see. The parish church dominated most villages and throughout the county the proximity of the manor house, with its private entrances into the church grounds and then into the church itself, was a regular feature. In the church the same divisions were often evident. Edward Miall wrote in 1849 that '... in Britain we carry our class distinctions into the house of God ... the poor man is made to feel that he is poor, and the rich is reminded that he is rich, in the great majority of our churches and chapels'. It is not difficult to imagine the scene at Syston when Sir John Thorold and his family attended church, arriving by carriage through private monumental gates directly from his estate. The seating arrangements often reflected the parish hierarchy. At Barton and Hackthorn the squire's pews were elevated not only to reflect his social position but so that he could monitor the rest of the congregation. At Leadenham, the Reeve family entered the church via an entrance from the house and sat in their own dedicated pews. It was usual for the family to enter last and leave first. Many of the landed class saw this as the natural order of rural society, as described in one verse, now seldom sung, of the popular hymn, 'All things bright and beautiful', written in 1849:

> The rich man in his castle
> The poor man at his gate
> God made them high and lowly
> And ordered their estate.

For many parishioners the argument for a return to Catholic ways was seen by many as irrelevant to their lives. Instead, the Church of England in Lincolnshire was faced not with what it regarded as the 'superstition' of Catholicism but the 'fanaticism' and what Bishop Wadesworth described in 1873 as the 'awful sin of schism' of nonconformity.

The Anglican church with its conservative hierarchical paternalism was seen to be failing to meet the spiritual needs of many working and labouring people. From the end of the 18th century this need was increasingly met by Methodism. For many followers Methodism became an important part of rural social control after the middle of the century when traditional paternalistic control of the squire was becoming less evident. Founded by John Wesley, the son of Samuel Wesley who was vicar of Epworth on the Isle of Axholme, Methodism's early development was not in Lincolnshire but in Bristol and the West Country. John's brother, Charles, who was also born at Epworth, wrote almost 7,000 hymns including some of the best known still sung today in the Christian tradition—'Jesus, Lover of My Soul', 'Hark the Herald Angels Sing', and 'Love Divine, All Loves Excelling'.

102 *John Wesley preaching at the Market Cross in Epworth.*

Throughout much of the 18th century John Wesley travelled extensively, preaching—often in open fields—his brand of Christianity based on the doctrines of Christian perfection and personal salvation through faith. Methodism began to gain popularity during the last quarter of the 18th century and most circuits were in place by 1825. By the Religious Census of 1851 there were 462 Wesleyan Methodist chapels in Lincolnshire. By this time Wesleyan Methodism had undergone its own schism and Primitive Methodism was formed at the beginning of the 19th century. This, too, grew quickly and by 1851 there were 221 Primitive Methodist chapels in the county, making Methodism by far the leading nonconformist group. Primitive Methodism developed a more evangelical approach to preaching and thus formed a more radical revivalist wing. The Wesleyan Methodists were quick to pass judgement. Their verdict on the Primitives was that they were '... of considerable mischief. And we disclaim all connection with them'. Despite this, Primitive Methodism came in 1809 to Grantham and Gainsborough. The former case is particularly interesting since it involved John Wedgwood, one of the famous Staffordshire potters. His name did not impress the authorities and he was arrested and imprisoned for preaching at the market cross at Grantham. Open-air preaching was a particular feature of early attempts to gain a foothold in the county. Many objected to the over zealous 'ranting' of the preachers, and many of them were met with insults and worse. When John Hallsworth preached for the first time at Lincoln he felt his life was in mortal danger from a mob. Similar experiences were reported by another preacher at both Waddington and Welbourn. At Holbeach the preacher was dragged off his chair and abused. Even so, converts were made. Preacher Thomas King visited Grimsby in 1819, where he delivered a sermon from a wheelbarrow; as a result of this unpromising start a new society was begun which soon occupied a disused chapel. At North Thoresby it was reported that within six months there were 80 members, 'most of whom have been noted for wickedness'. Evangelical zeal on the part of the preachers was evident at Louth, where 'the devil was forced to fly and the sinners cried out for mercy'. By the middle of the century most Lincolnshire towns could boast a variety of dissenting chapels. For

example, the 1856 White's *Directory* indicates six dissenting religions vying for congregations in Gainsborough. The Roman Catholics were described as having a 'small place of worship'; the Wesleyan Chapel had been built in 1804 and had seating for 1,000; a Primitive Methodist Chapel was built in 1838 and an Independent Chapel in 1821. There was also a Unitarian Chapel and a 'small' Friends' Meeting House which dated from the beginning of the 18th century. At the smaller market town of Market Rasen there was a Roman Catholic Chapel established in 1823; a large Wesleyan Chapel built in 1838, when the old chapel, which had been built in 1800, was taken over by the Primitive Methodists. There was also a Free Methodist Chapel, built in 1852.

The 1851 Religious Census reveals that the Church of England attendance was highest at the morning and afternoon services and Methodist attendance greatest in the evening. This can partly be accounted for by dual attendance—at both the Anglican church in the morning/afternoon and at nonconformist chapel in the evening. At Nocton, for example, the Rev. Hobart noted that some of his congregation were 'known to be regular dissenters'. This pattern was repeated throughout Lincolnshire. Methodism was particularly strong in the north west of the county around Thorne, and to a lesser extent in the parishes around Caistor, Brigg, and Louth, where the morning and afternoon services were equally well attended. In the Grantham area and around Stamford Anglicanism remained most influential. Although after the 1851 Census of Religious Worship tremendous concern was expressed about the

103 *The Methodist chapel, New York.*

national decline in church attendance, this was mainly directed at the growing industrial cities. In a rural county such as Lincolnshire church attendance remained relatively high.

Attitudes amongst landowners to Methodism varied. Some landowners who were dominant in a parish could, if they chose to, prevent Dissenter chapels being erected. In 1866 the Primitive Methodists at Welby obtained a piece of land from the dominant landowner, Sir G.E. Welby, on which to build their chapel after having used a farmhouse kitchen for 70 years. The use of cottages for worship was quite frequent and congregations were willing to travel between parishes to attend. Similarly, Earl Dysart granted a piece of land at Great Ponton for the construction of a chapel. Such a liberal attitude was not always the case. At Welbourn, the Countess of Buckinghamshire, the dominant landowner, threatened one of her tenants with the loss of his farm if he did not stop using a barn for preaching. By contrast, Lord Yarborough, the largest landowner in Lincolnshire, was prepared to tolerate Dissenter chapels on his Lindsey estate because he saw Methodists as sober and industrious. In 1841 he had 12 Wesleyan chapels on his estate and had given permission for land to be let at minimal rent for a Primitive Methodist chapel at Keelby. The steward of the Brocklesby estate was reported to have said that Methodists were 'some of the best tenants Lord Yarborough has'. The attitude of parish priests to Methodism also varied and was often dependent on where the individual stood in the high church, low church debate. At Bardney there was much co-operation between the

104 *Methodist chapel at Theddlethorpe St Helen.*

two; the Sunday School used the Wesleyan Chapel one week and the parish church the next. At Ingham the school room was administered by equal numbers of trustees from the parish church, the Wesleyan and Primitive Methodist chapels. This level of integration was, however, unusual. For the majority of clergy the existence of an active chapel in 'their' parish was seen at best as an irritation and, at worst, a direct challenge to the traditional position of the established church in the lives of the people. In Lusby the majority of the parishioners were described as either 'actual Dissenters or constant attendants [*sic*] at the Methodist chapel'; the population of South Willingham consisted almost entirely of Wesleyan Methodists and the rector of Donington reported that there was not 'a single person whom I can designate a member of the Church of England'.

Methodist chapels come in all sizes. Early chapels were often only meagre single red-brick rooms. Many of them can still be seen today around the county and reflect not only the small congregations but also the style of worship. However, in larger villages and towns they were able to build impressive chapels. In the large parishes of Bassingham, Billinghay and Great Hale, for example, there were thriving dissenting congregations. In 1839 at Bassingham the Wesleyans built a 'handsome structure, at a cost of £1,000, and went on to build a school in 1855 costing £650 raised largely by subscription. In Billinghay there were three chapels; a Wesleyan chapel built in 1832, a Baptist built in 1847 and a Primitive Methodist built in 1850; at Great Hale the Wesleyan chapel was replaced by a new Primitive Methodist chapel in 1851. However, in the towns the evidence for the size of congregations and the confidence of Methodists during the second half of the century can best be seen. At Lincoln, for example, a Wesleyan chapel was built in Clasketgate in 1836, followed by the magnificent neo-classical Hannah Memorial Chapel on the High Street in 1864 and St Catherine's and Bailgate in 1880. The impact of nonconformity was such that in 1886 Bishop King summed up the results of his first visitation returns as 'Dissent! Dissent! Dissent!'

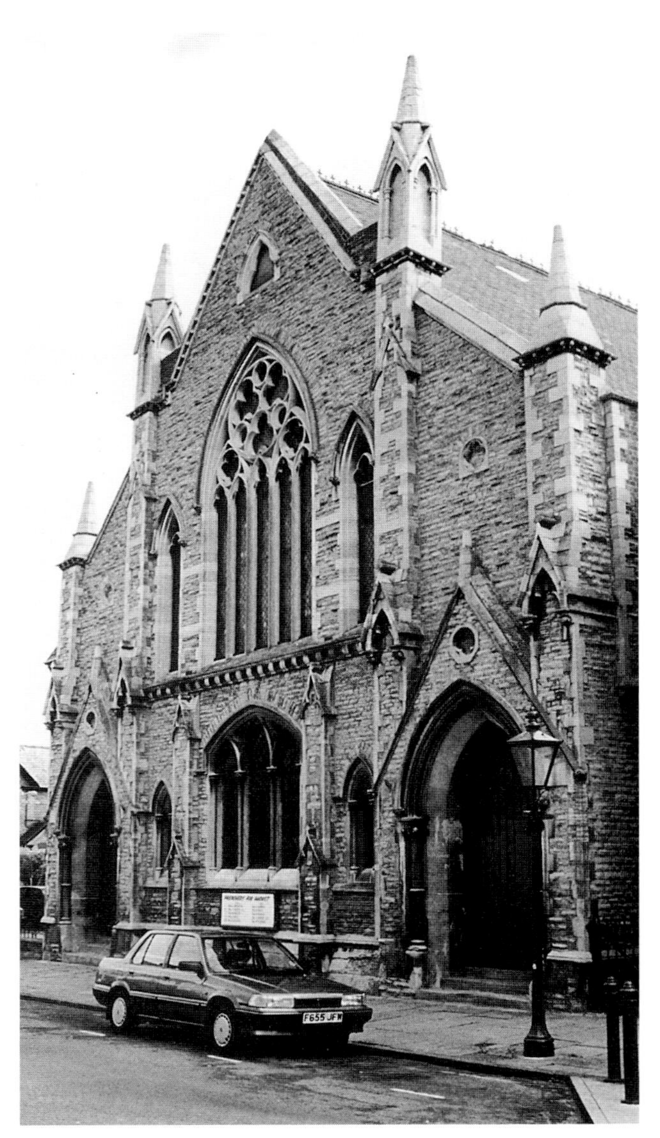

105 *Bailgate Methodist church, Lincoln.*

17

Defence of the Realm—RAF Lincolnshire

The Royal Air Force and the county of Lincolnshire are synonymous. During both world wars and the 'Cold War', Lincolnshire has been at the centre of the country's defence and in today's post-Cold War world the county remains an important cog in the air defence of Britain and in Britain's wider role in NATO. A rural setting, large areas of flat land and its eastern location has made it an ideal site for airfields. At the height of RAF activity during the Second World War in the region of 30,000 acres (12,145 ha) of the county were given over to RAF stations, nearly all located on the well-drained chalk and limestone uplands. This was arguably the greatest impact on the landscape since the enclosures of the 18th and 19th centuries. Not only have the hardware of hangars, runways and married quarters had an impact on the county but so too have the personnel. The impact on the local economy of thousands of servicemen and women and their families has been enormous. Moreover, there is a less tangible, but nevertheless real affinity with the RAF in the county amongst a large section of the non-service population.

Although the RAF began officially on 1 April 1918, its predecessors the Royal Flying Corp (RFC), a branch of the army, and the Royal Naval Air Service (RNAS) had both operated from the county for much of the First World War and, by 1918, some 37 military airfields were in use. Most, however, were little more than cleared fields that had been grassed to provide a runway. Leadenham, for example, was only 86 acres. Only seven aerodromes could be described as 'Operational', whereas 13 were Emergency Landing Grounds, an indication that in those early days, flying was still precarious. At that time, because of the temporary nature of most airfields, their function was easily changed. That there were operational airfields in the county suggests a perceived threat which had to be met. Indeed, the First World War saw Zeppelin raids which caused a public outcry. Some damage was done—for example at Cleethorpes in 1916—and aircraft were scrambled on a number of occasions, from the RNAS at Killingholme and Cranwell and the RFC Home Defence Squadrons from Leadenham, Scampton, Kirton, Gainsborough, Elsham, Buckminster and Tydd St Mary. At the end of the war the number of aerodromes was quickly reduced, so that by the beginning of 1920 there was just a handful. The most important function of these bases in the inter-war period was training. This centred on Royal Air Force College Cranwell for both flying training and apprentice

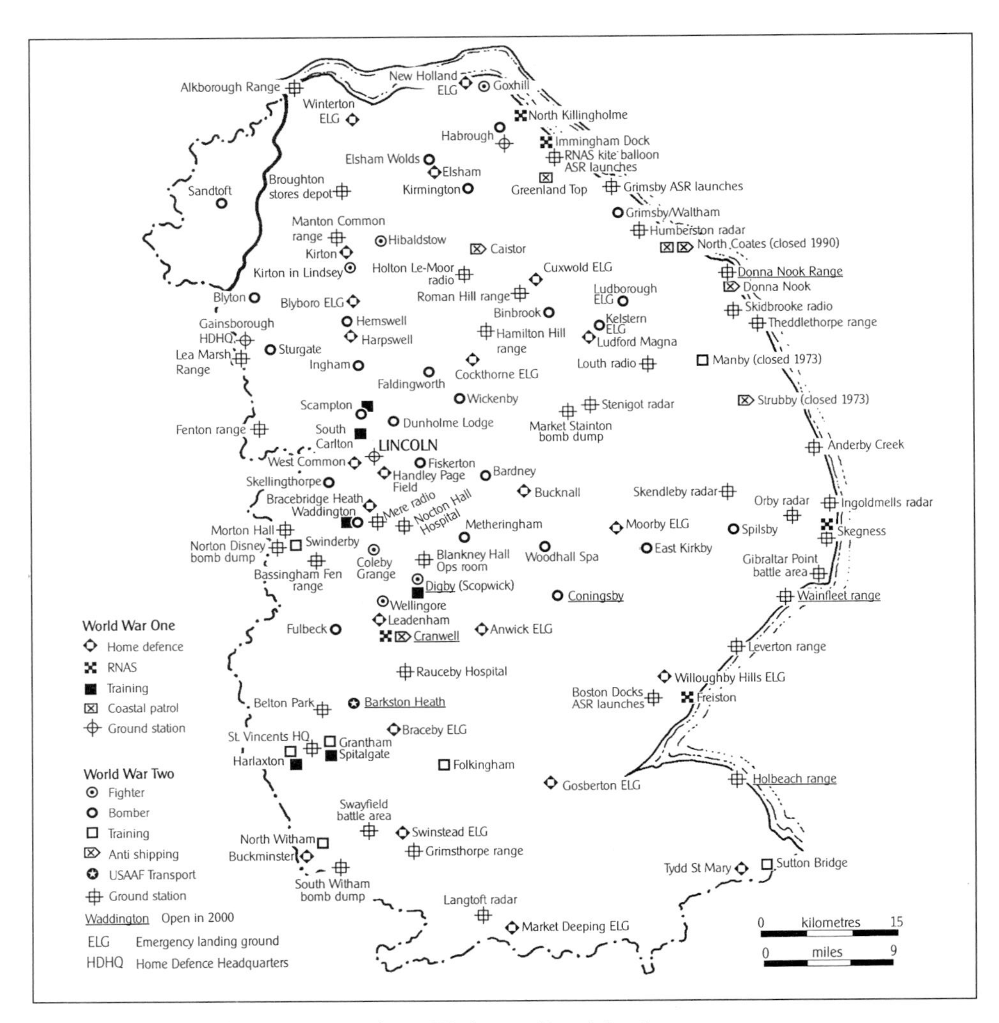

106 *The RAF in Lincolnshire.*

training, until the Apprentice School was moved to Halton, Buckinghamshire in 1926. A sparsely populated county with large areas of flat land, with coastal sites such as Donna Nook and Holbeach bombing ranges, Lincolnshire was ideal for flying training. Pilots were also trained at Digby and Grantham, while North Coates and Sutton Bridge were used for armaments training. Waddington was reopened in 1926 and became the home of Lincoln's Auxiliary Air Force Squadron.

The darkening war clouds of the 1930s brought a change in the function of RAF stations and during the Second World War Lincolnshire's role became increasingly important as the offensive bombing campaign grew. Bombers from the county could reach Germany and occupied Europe. Conversely, the Luftwaffe could reach Lincolnshire, and therefore fighter squadrons had to be stationed at Digby, Wellingore, Coleby Grange to the south of Lincoln, and Kirton-in-Lindsey and Hibaldstow in the north to intercept German bombers and defend the

107 *The Lancaster was the main RAF heavy bomber of the Second World War.*

airfields. Aircraft also flew out over the North Sea on convoy patrols. However, the county is best known for bombers. In March 1943 there were 11 bomber stations in the county, rising to 29 bases operating Avro Lancasters in April 1945, and the name 'bomber county' remains today. Lincolnshire, therefore, played a most important part in the defeat of Nazi Germany, especially from 1942 when the bombing offensive increased. It was not uncommon to see the sky over Lincolnshire filled with Lancasters *en route* to form part of the 1,000 bomber sorties over Germany. The first such raid was on Cologne in May 1942. Other raids were more specialised. On 16 May 1943, under the code name Operation Chastise, 18 Lancasters of 617 Squadron took off from RAF Scampton under the leadership of Wing Commander Guy Gibson to attack the Mohne, Eider and Sorpe dams in an attempt to flood and destroy the industries of the Ruhr valley.

108 *The memorial at RAF Wickenby.*

Bombing raids were made almost nightly, weather permitting, and enormous losses were suffered by bomber crews. The memorial book in the Services Chapel in Lincoln Cathedral lists more than 25,000 names of airmen killed in action from airfields in or near Lincolnshire. The worst night was that of 30 March 1944 when 381 aircraft were sent from Lincolnshire and 44 failed to return, lost over Nuremberg. Many memorials are to be found in the county; one example is at the entrance to what used to be RAF Wickenby, in memory of the Canadian, Australian, New Zealander as well as British airmen. Wickenby was part of No. 1 Group Bomber Command between 1942

and 1945, flying firstly Vickers Armstrong Wellingtons, later Avro Lancasters and, lastly, the DeHavilland Mosquito. The memorial reads:

> In Memory of the One Thousand and Eighty Men of 12 and 626 Squadrons who Gave Their Lives on Operations from This Airfield in the Offensive against Germany and the Liberation of Occupied Europe.

Although the United States played a vital part in the bombing campaign, most US bombers flew from East Anglian bases. Its principal base in Lincolnshire from 1943 was at Goxhill, where it was mainly involved in training future bomber crews. The other US operations from Barkston, Folkingham and North Witham and, in a limited way, from Fulbeck were in troop-carrying C47 Dakotas and gliders which were to play such important parts both in the 1944 Normandy landings and the attacks on the Rhine bridges at Arnhem in Holland by the Parachute Regiment.

By 1943, the threat of daytime bombing by the Luftwaffe had receded. Thus the need for fighter support was reduced and a number of stations became training stations for foreign squadrons; for example, there were Poles at Kirton-in-Lindsey and Canadians and later Czechs at Digby. Night attacks remained a problem, and a Canadian squadron was responsible for this, operating for the latter part of the war from Coleby Grange. Because of the long coastline, radar installations were built at Orby, Langtoft, Stenigot, Ingoldmells and Skendleby, while North Coates and Strubby became centres for attacking enemy shipping in the North Sea. The county also played an important role in the development of the turbojet engine during this period, although the first operational jet aircraft only saw service towards the end of the war, against German flying bombs. Invented by Frank Whittle, the first British jet-powered aircraft flew from RAF Cranwell in May 1941.

With the end of the war came an enormous and almost immediate cut-back in the number of RAF stations as service personnel were demobilised. By 1946 only Binbrook, Kirton-in-Lindsey, Manby, Sturgate, Sutton Bridge, Metheringham, North Coates, Scampton, Skellingthorpe, Spilsby, Swinderby and Waddington were still active airfields. Although the German threat had gone, the Berlin blockade revealed a new threat from the Soviet Union. As the Cold War developed the county's position on the east of the

109 *An American Lockheed Lightning at Goxhill in 1944.*

110 *The Vulcan was once responsible for delivering Britain's nuclear deterrent.*

country left it in the forefront of Britain's defence. After 1955 Britain became a nuclear power, relying on the RAF and its new nuclear strike force of 'V Bombers' to deliver the atom and later hydrogen bombs to the target. Three new bombers were brought into service—the Handley Page Victor, the Vickers Valiant and the Avro Vulcan—and the latter was stationed in Lincolnshire at Waddington and Scampton. The first Vulcan arrived in 1956. By 1960, however, the emphasis of nuclear deterrence had passed to missile delivery systems in the form of American Thor ICBMs, some of which were located in the county at six sites—Hemswell, Bardney, Caistor, Coleby Grange, Ludford and Folkingham. This policy was short-lived and, by 1963, had been abandoned in favour of aircraft delivery systems, which in turn came to an end in 1969 when the nuclear deterrent role was taken on by the Royal Navy's Polaris fleet. The location of ICBMs and bomber bases in the county meant that fighter aircraft—such as the Gloster Javelin initially, then the thoroughbred English Electric Lightnings and US-made McDonnell Phantoms—were stationed in the county. On many occasions, Lightnings from RAF Binbrook and Phantoms from RAF Coningsby were scrambled to intercept Soviet bombers over the North Sea as they continually probed Britain's air defence systems in a cat and mouse game of the Cold War.

During the post-war period the county consolidated its position for training RAF personnel. For much of this time flying training was carried on at Manby, Strubby, Swinderby and Cranwell, although all flying training in the county now takes place at the Royal Air Force College Cranwell. During the mid-1960s Swinderby was taken over for all RAF recruit training. As the Cold War in effect ended with the dismantling of the Soviet Union and the Warsaw Pact, the so-called 'peace dividend' has inevitably affected the county. By the latter part of the 1980s most RAF stations had closed and at the end of the 20th century only Cranwell for officer and flying training (with a satellite at Barkston Heath), Digby as a signal centre, Coningsby conversion unit operating Tornado fighters in an air defence role, and Waddington operating AWACS Sentry flying radar stations remain open. The coastal bombing ranges at Holbeach, Wainfleet and Donna Nook are still operating and a new air warfare training facility has been established off the Lincolnshire coast, which is used by European airforces as well as the RAF.

The RAF has had a very important economic impact on the county. Thousands of personnel on regular wages have helped to support local business. Initially, however, servicemen and women lived on camps which were relatively self-sufficient, providing their own entertainment in the form of ASTRA camp cinemas, with Officers', Sergeants' and Airmen's Messes, and their own accommodation—billets for single men and women or 'married quarters'. Service wages reflected this 'all-found' nature of service life. Money spent outside the camp was limited, nor was there

much opportunity for the employment of local people since most jobs were filled by RAF personnel, though work opportunities were found for local contractors and tradesmen in the construction of runways and building works at RAF stations and as accommodation was modernised. By the mid-1960s this was beginning to change; Britain pulled back from east of Suez and colonies gained their independence, so there was a reduction in the RAF's commitment. After the end of National Service, there was more stability in service life and personnel were less liable to frequent postings. Many servicemen began to buy houses away from the camp, and an influx of service personnel into villages made an impact on the local economy. Not only did house prices rise but also new houses were built. The market town of Sleaford, and villages such as Scopwick, Ruskington, Tattershall and Leasingham, expanded as a result. Because of its proximity to RAF Scampton, Welton was known locally as 'RAF Welton'. In the early 1980s, 30 per cent of children attending the William Farr Comprehensive School at Welton and 38 per cent at the Gartree School at Tattershall were from service families.

The end of National Service in 1960 provided more opportunities for employment on RAF stations when jobs such as secretaries and drivers could be filled by civilians. This was boosted during the 1980s with the policy of the Conservative government to privatise many jobs which had been undertaken by servicemen and women. For example, all aircraft maintenance at RAF Cranwell was taken over by Airworks Ltd. although it relied heavily on ex-RAF personnel.

The name 'bomber county' cannot now truthfully be applied to Lincolnshire since the era of the bombers ended with the final flight of the Vulcan from Waddington in 1984 although one was retained for display purposes until 1993. For many people, however, it is a name that will endure for a long time in the memory, evoked by the sound of the four Rolls-Royce Merlin engines of the last surviving Lancaster in the Battle of Britain Memorial Flight, based at RAF Coningsby.

111 *AWACS Sentry aircraft at RAF Waddington.*

18

The Twentieth Century

In 1901 the population of the historic county of Lincolnshire, from the river Humber in the north to the Wash in the south, was 500,022. By the end of the 20th century it had risen to approximately 929,250, an increase of 86 percent. By this time Lincolnshire had become three separate counties, Lindsey, Kesteven and Holland, each administered by a county council. The City of Lincoln was also made a discrete administrative unit as a county borough. By the end of the 19th century Grimsby had also achieved county borough status. The division of Lincolnshire into four administrative units under the Local Government Act 1888 formalised what had been evolving since the Middle Ages. By the 19th century local government was in the hands of magistrates acting in Quarter Sessions, where they not only had a judicial function but an administrative role, which developed during the century. The passing of the 1867 Reform Act demonstrated the need for democratic control of local affairs. Through much of the 20th century the County, Borough, Urban District and Rural District Councils provided the ever increasing number of services for all of Lincolnshire. However, in 1974 local government reorganisation created the new county of Humberside, in which most of north Lindsey became South Humberside, and a new county of Lincolnshire with its headquarters at Lincoln. South Lindsey, Kesteven and Holland still functioned, but were divided into district councils with reduced powers. From the outset Humberside was unpopular both with residents in what had been Lindsey and with those on the north bank of the river Humber in what had been the East Riding of Yorkshire. In 1996 under further local government reorganisation South Humberside was abolished and returned to Lincolnshire, but not to a united county despite popular demand for 'Lincolnshire—From the Humber to the Wash'. Instead the county is divided into three unitary authorities: Scunthorpe and Brigg form North Lincolnshire, and Grimsby and Cleethorpes have become North East Lincolnshire. Thus at the beginning of the 21st century Lincolnshire remains as it has been through most of its history, a region rather than a single administrative unit.

The population of rural parishes continued the decline begun during the last quarter of the 19th century, albeit at a slower rate, as efficiencies led to fewer being employed on the land. The area with the most sustained drop in population up to the middle of the 20th century has been the

small parishes of the central and southern Wolds and central and southern Kesteven. On the other hand, the population of most fen parishes and those on the north-eastern coastal marshes has generally increased. Urban areas and those associated with specific industries—Grimsby and Boston with their ports, the holiday industry at Skegness and steel production in and around Scunthorpe, and RAF stations at Waddington, Coningsby and Cranwell—have all shown substantial increases. Personal mobility has also reversed the decline and many villages have become 'dormitories' for urban or industrial centres. In the south of the county, Bourne, Market Deeping, Deeping St James and Langtoft have undergone enormous population increase in the last 25 years due to the growth of nearby Peterborough and the connection with the main east-coast railway.

Lincolnshire remains predominantly agricultural though the rate of change has increased just as in other areas of the country. Those visiting the county see thousands of acres of land given over to food production. Compared with city life, rural Lincolnshire may represent a nostalgic ideal. However, agricultural production over the last century has undergone a revolution, making Lincolnshire one of the most highly 'industrialised' and productive areas in the entire country. There is very little natural landscape in Lincolnshire. Even woodland is managed. Ninety per cent of the county is given over to farming compared with 77 per cent for the whole country. Other national comparisons are worth making. Lincolnshire contains some of the best quality soils, with 44 percent at Grade 1 and 2 (out of 5), compared with an average of 16 per cent for England. Superior soils, a favourable topography and climate have combined to ensure the dominance of agriculture into the 21st century.

In 1900, however, farming was in the doldrums. The impact of the most severe agricultural depression ever experienced in English farming was still evident. Those parishes on the heavy clays and upland farms of the Wolds and Heath were most badly affected, and, despite the demand created by the First World War, continued in a depressed state into the 1930s. By comparison, the low-lying fenland areas remained relatively prosperous, because there farmers could diversify into a wider range of marketable crops; for example, market gardening, pea production for canning and bulb production in South Holland. The period up to the Second World War saw fundamental changes in farming practices in the county as farmers had to grapple with new economic circumstances. The acreage producing wheat increased by 60 per cent, almost matched by a reduction of just under 48 per cent in the production of barley. As the number of horses required on the land (and elsewhere) declined, so did the cultivation of oats. The number of sheep, such an important part of the county's rural scene for centuries, also declined from just over a million at the beginning of the century to about half that number in 1937.

The Second World War caused a tremendous change in the fortunes of agriculture. The production of foodstuffs became a question of national survival and Lincolnshire, as one of the principal arable areas, was at the forefront of this battle. War Agricultural Committees, largely under the

LINCOLNSHIRE COUNTY COUNCIL

112 *The three 'Lincolnshire' council logos.*

control of farmers with draconian powers to compel compliance, were made responsible for the direction of farming to meet national demands and to distribute the various subsidies for improvements. The effect was to increase the land under the plough at the expense of grasslands with a subsequent reduction in stock-keeping. Farm work was a reserved occupation, but many chose to join the forces or work in munitions causing a shortage of labour, partly answered by nearly 2,000 members of the Women's Land Army, 1,850 prisoners of war and an increase in mechanisation. For example, the number of tractors increased from 7,119 in 1942 to 9,667 in 1944. Marshall, Son & Co. Ltd. of Gainsborough built some 2,000 threshing machines, representing more than half the total made during the war.

After the war, agriculture entered a new golden age, a result of successive government policies to maintain a good supply of food cheaply to the consumer, of mechanisation and of the increase in scientific understanding of chemical fertilisers. At the end of the 20th century, approximately 75 per cent of Lincolnshire's land is under the plough; the production of wheat and barley is roughly equal, and 12 per cent is grassland and rough grazing. The demand for increased production has been so great that the introduction of larger machines has also meant larger fields in which to operate. Hedgerows have been torn down, resulting in an altered landscape. Much of the war-time organisation survived into the post-war period, greater efficiency being achieved through marketing boards such as the Milk Marketing Board and the Potato Marketing Board or 'self help' groups like the Farmers' Meat Corporation. Sugar beet was processed by the British Sugar Corporation at Brigg, Bardney or Spalding or just outside the county at King's Lynn, Newark, or Ely. Vegetables are produced for freezing. Following the demise of the deep-sea fishing industry at Grimsby there has been diversification into food processing, and major employers in the town include Ross-Young, Birdseye-Walls and Blue Crest, for freezing both vegetables and fish. Twenty per cent of Britain's fish is still processed at Grimsby and the town produces more frozen pizzas than anywhere else. In South Holland the food processing is equally important. At Spalding, Geest's, who sold their banana business in 1996, are involved with the large-scale production and distribution of flowers and chilled foods. Nationally known companies such as Haywood's and Lockwood's pre-packed foods are now part of HL Foods, based at Little Sutton. Distribution is also an important part of the local economy, undertaken by companies such as Leverton's of Spalding. By the early 1970s the once extensive malting industry for brewing (in 1856 there were 163 maltsters in Lincolnshire) had been concentrated at Grantham.

113 *New farming technology. A tractor and binder at Whitton in 1936.*

There is now only one major brewer, Bateman's Brewery which operates at Wainfleet.

Agriculture was given a boost by the Common Agricultural Policy of the EEC (EU) after Britain joined in 1973 with the aim both of guaranteeing a strategic supply of food and reducing fluctuations in the market and subsequently farm income caused by the cyclical nature of agricultural production. The result was to stabilise prices and ensure a minimum return to the farmer, whilst at the same making certain of the supply of food to the consumers at a reasonable price. Production has been at an all time high and the EU has had to intervene to buy surpluses. This policy has been highly controversial and radical solutions have thus been sought. In 1993 some ten per cent of farm land was set-a-side. The agricultural industry is leaving the 20th century as it entered it, in a depression. The reduction of subsidies, the change to the structure of the various purchasing agencies, and public concern about food safety have all combined to ensure a difficult time ahead for the county's farmers.

Heavy engineering still exists in the county albeit in a much more reduced form than at the beginning of the century. On the eve of the First World War a buoyant manufacturing sector—Clayton & Shuttleworth Ltd.; Robey & Co. Ltd.; William Fosters Ltd.; Clarkes Crank & Forge Co. Ltd. and Ruston Proctor & Co. Ltd.—occupied the narrow Lincoln Gap. Richard Hornsby & Sons were at Grantham, Rose Brothers Ltd. and Marshall & Sons Co. Ltd. were at Gainsborough and Blackstone & Co. Ltd. were at Stamford. These were substantial employers. Not to be forgotten is the Scunthorpe iron and steel industry which at the beginning of the century consisted of five independent producers. However, in the mid-1930s three of them were amalgamated into the mighty Appleby-Frodingham Steel Company until 1953 when they were all nationalised. The reason for the location of these iron and steel works was their proximity to iron ore at Frodingham. This had been mined in the 19th century and continued into the 20th century, becoming particularly important during wartime when other sources were unavailable. There were quarries in other parts of the county, particularly on the limestone ridge north and south of Grantham on the Lincolnshire/Leicestershire border, fed by specially built mineral railways on the existing network through Lincoln and onto Scunthorpe.

The First World War gave a tremendous boost to the county's engineering industry. Lincoln became one of the major aircraft producers: for example, Ruston Proctor alone built over 2,000 aircraft and 3,000 engines. Robey's and Clayton & Shuttleworth in Lincoln and Marshall's at Gainsborough were also aircraft producers. So many aircraft were produced that Lincoln's West Common was temporarily made into a landing strip and a new aerodrome was built at Bracebridge Heath for testing aircraft before delivery to their operational units. The entire county's engineering industry was on a war footing, producing guns, shells and gun mountings. The county is best known for the production of the first tanks. These, code named 'water carriers for Mesopotamia', were developed in

the Lincoln factory of W. Foster's under the managing director William Tritton. The prototype was tested at Burton, north of Lincoln, at the end of 1915. Much changed, it entered service on the Western Front, at first unsuccessfully in the Battle of Cambrai. This was not the fault of the tank, although, of the 378 tanks deployed, 71 broke down and 43 got stuck in ditches. Their use later in the war was much more successful.

The growth and success of Lincolnshire's heavy engineering came to a sudden decline at the end of the war. The industry which had dedicated itself to war-time production was no longer needed and the dislocation of trade at the end of the war made it impossible to rekindle pre-war contracts. The Russian Revolution caused a number of the county's engineering firms to lose investments made there before 1917. Some companies were quick to see that government contracts would soon come to an end. By the end of 1918 Richard Hornsby & Son Ltd. had amalgamated with Ruston, Proctor & Co. Ltd. to become Ruston & Hornsby Ltd. who, for a short time, produced cars. Others fared less well by failing to respond to changing markets. Clayton and Shuttleworth Ltd. remained committed to the production of steam wagons which were very successful until the technology was surpassed by the internal combustion engine; the company was wound up in 1930 at the height of the depression. In such a time of commercial uncertainty, mergers of profitable parts of companies were frequent. In this way Thomas Smith of Coventry purchased the Clayton Forge to form Smith Clayton Forge.

The Second World War brought new contracts for Lincolnshire engineering works. Prominent were the diesel engines for locomotives produced by Ruston and Hornsby. They also continued the production of tanks begun by Foster's during the First World War. At Grantham, Aveling-Barford who had close commercial connections with Ruston's, was formed in 1933 and built tanks and machine-gun carriers. Also millions of rounds of ammunition were produced at Grantham which attracted the attention of German bombers between 1940 and 1942. Other factories throughout Lincolnshire were producing a multitude of component parts for the war machine.

Since 1945 the engineering picture in the county has been characterised by merger and take over, so that now only one company, Smith Clayton Forge, is a link with those that existed in 1914, although Foster & Co. Ltd. was the only large-scale company actually to leave the county. Soon after the war Ruston & Hornsby started producing industrial gas turbines and by the early 1970s they were the leading producer in Britain and major exporters. In 1961 they were taken over by English Electric Co. Ltd., part of General Electric Co. Ltd. (GEC), to form Ruston Gas Turbines. At the beginning of the 21st century they continue to produce gas turbines for the home and export markets under the name of Alstom.

In recent years the county has been an oil producer. The first workable deposits were found in 1943 at Nocton but it was not until the early 1980s, when oil was discovered at Welton, Nettleham, Stainton and Scampton, that the beam pumps or 'nodding donkeys' appeared on

114 *Farming at the end of the 20th century: a combine harvester.*

the landscape. An oil gathering centre has been built at Welton with a rail link to a refinery on Humberside. At about 4,000 barrels a day, production is relatively small, but it is enough to be economically viable. In the Gainsborough area the gas by-product of the oil exploration has been used to heat the local swimming pool, secondary school, industrial and residential estates. Whereas oil has been sought, the vast reserves of coal which extend into Lincolnshire from the east Nottinghamshire and, to a lesser extent, the north-east Leicestershire coalfields remain untapped. The retraction of the British coal industry and cheap imports mean these are unlikely to be worked. Off-shore exploration has also affected the county. In 1972 the Viking North Sea Gas terminal was built at Theddlethorpe, which receives gas from more than 20 platforms located in the North Sea. Much of this gas passes through pipelines beneath the Lincolnshire countryside to a number of inland distribution points. Immingham's King's Dock, which, as Grimsby's Royal Dock half a century earlier, was promoted by railway investment, was opened in 1912 and has developed into a major facility. As well as two oil refineries it handles chemicals, fertilisers, grain and roll on-roll off traffic. At Boston the docks import steel from Russia and very large quantities of timber from the traditional source of Scandinavia. Much of this timber is destined for the building trade and for telephone poles.

The quality of roads in the county remains a problem. A look at a road atlas shows only one motorway, the M180, which connects the more industrial northern parts of the county, including Scunthorpe, Grimsby and Immingham, with links to the Humber Bridge and to the motorway network. The Humber Bridge, with a span of 1,410 metres,

115 *'Nodding Donkey'.*

was opened in 1981 not only to join the north and south bank of the river Humber physically, but also to help consolidate politically the new Humberside County Council. There were also plans to extend the M11 from Cambridge northwards, passing Long Sutton, Coningsby, Market Rasen and then to the Humber Bridge. The importance to commerce of good roads is paramount. That the enormous Christian Salvesen frozen food distribution store is at Easton is because of its proximity to the A1. During the last decade of the 20th century a new link which bypasses villages and Spalding has been built to improve connections between the A1 at Peterborough and Boston. The county not only had just one motorway, but it has few dual carriageways. Local councils and commercial interests in Lincoln have for a number of years been lobbying to make the Fosse Way (A46) from the A1 at Newark into a dual carriageway. For the most part, however, improvements to the county's road system have been made through straightening bends and bypassing towns and villages. Thus over the last 25 years, for example, the main trunk road, the A17, from King's Lynn to Newark has been much improved.

Tourism in the county has been growing for a number of years and is becoming increasingly important. New hotels are being built. Day tripping to the coast is still popular and, for example, Skegness, Cleethorpes and Mablethorpe still attract thousands of holidaymakers. 'Fantasy Island', at Ingoldmells, a new concept in all-weather attractions, was opened in 1995 and Butlin's Family Resort Centre at Ingoldmells was refurbished in 1999 and now caters for approximately 10,000 people per week. Other areas of the county also attract more tourists. Both the Fens and the Wolds have their own appeal catering for the interests of increasing numbers, but Lincoln remains the main magnet for foreign tourists. Whatever their reasons for visiting, they find a county full of historical interest.

Select Bibliography

Ambler, R.W., *Ranters Revivalists and Reformers*, 1989
Beastall, T.W., *The Agricultural Revolution in Lincolnshire*, 1978
Beckwith, I., *The Book of Lincoln*, 1990
Bennett, S., Bennett, N., (eds.) *An Historical Atlas of Lincolnshire*, 1993
Darby, H.C., *The Draining of the Fens*, 1940
Grigg, D., *The Agricultural Revolution in South Lincolnshire*, 1966
Hadfield, C., *The Canals of the East Midlands*, 1966
Hancock, T.N., *Bomber County*, 1978
Hancock, T.N., *Bomber County 2*, 1985
Hill, Sir Francis, *Medieval Lincoln*, 1948
Hill, Sir Francis, *Tudor and Stuart Lincoln*, 1956
Hill, Sir Francis, *Georgian Lincoln*, 1966
Hill, Sir Francis, *Victorian Lincoln*, 1974
Hodgett, G., *Tudor Lincolnshire*, 1975
Holmes, Charles, *Seventeenth Century Lincolnshire*, 1980
Honeybone, M., *The Book of Grantham*, 1980
Jones, M.J., *Lincoln—History and Guide*, 1993
Kaye, D., *The Book of Grimsby*, 1981
Leahy, K. and Williams, D., *North Lincolnshire: A Pictorial History*, 1996
Leary, William, *Lincolnshire Methodism*, 1988
May, J., *Pre-historic Lincolnshire*, 1976
Morgan, P. and Thorn, C., Domesday Book: *Lincolnshire*, Vol.1 & 2, 1896
Obelkevich, J., *Religion and Rural Society in South Lincolnshire, 1825-1875*, 1976
Olney, R.J., *Rural Society and County Government in Nineteenth Century Lincolnshire*, 1979
Owen, Dorothy M., *Church and Society in Medieval Lincolnshire*, 1990
Pevsner, N. Harris, J., *The Buildings of England: Lincolnshire*, 1964
Platt, G., *Land and People in Medieval Lincolnshire*, 1985
Robinson, D.N., *The Book of Louth*, 1979
Robinson, D.N., *The Book of the Lincolnshire Seaside*, 1981
Rogers, A., *The Book of Stamford*, 1983
Ruddock, J.G. and Pearson, R.E., Railway History of Lincoln, 1974
Russell, Rex C., *The Logic of the Open Field System*, n.d.

Russell, Rex C., *The Enclosure of Holton le Clay, 1763-1766, Waltham 1769-1771, and Tetney, 1774-1779*, 1972
Swayer, P., *Anglo-Saxon Lincolnshire*, 1998
Thirsk, J., *English Peasant Farming*, 1957
Varley, Joan, *The Parts of Kesteven*, 1974
Victoria County History of Lincolnshire, 1906
Vince, A. (ed.), *Pre-Viking Lindsey*, 1993
Wheeler, W.H., *A History of the Fens of South Lincolnshire*, 1896
White, W., *History, Gazetteer, and Directory of Lincolnshire*, 1856
Whitwell, J.B., *Roman Lincolnshire*, 1992
Wright, N.R., *Lincolnshire Towns and Industry, 1700-1914*, 1982
Young, A., *General View of the Agriculture of the County of Lincolnshire*, 1813

Index

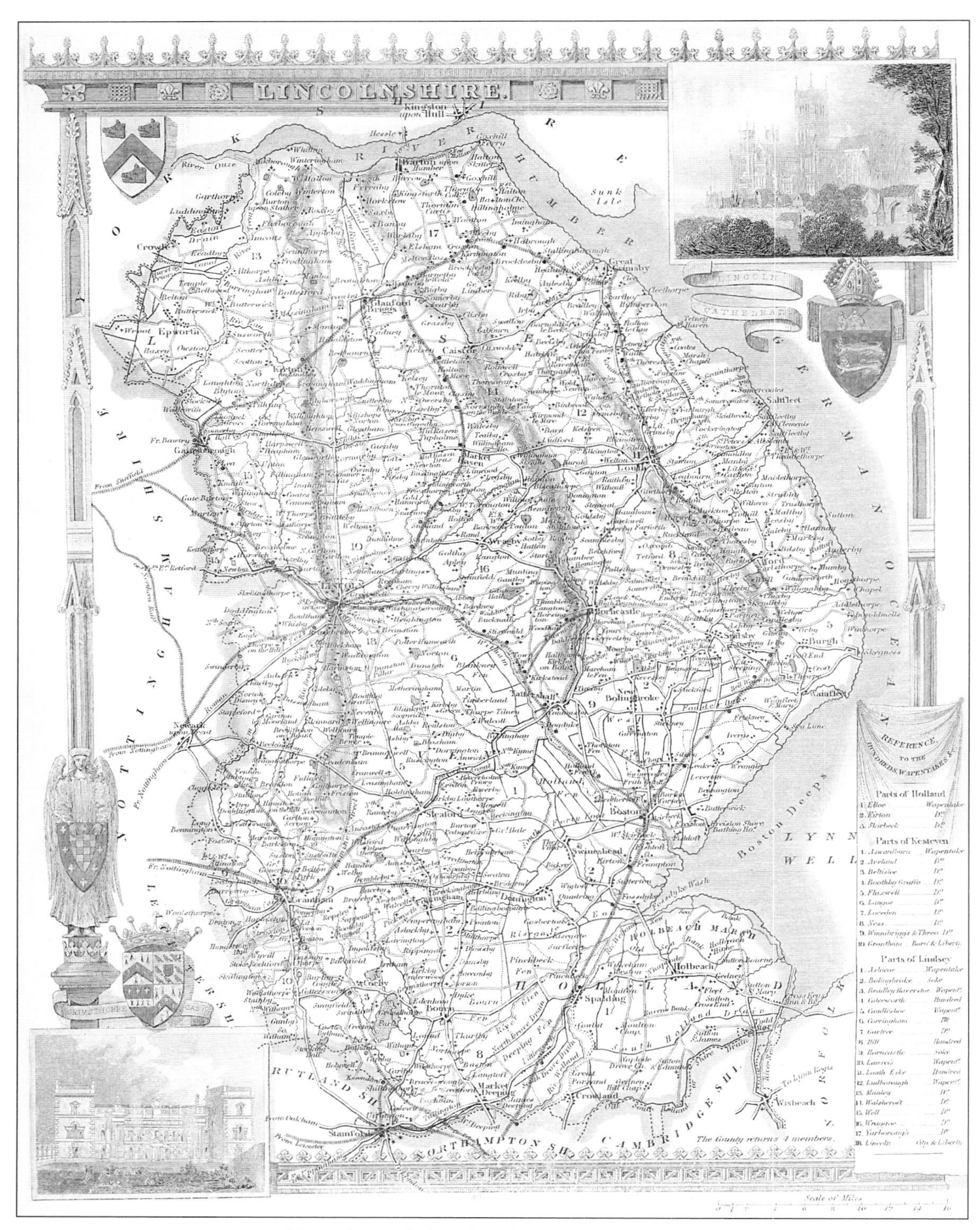

Map of Lincolnshire by Thomas Moule, c.1840.